An Island In
Grand Traverse Bay

Author Kathleen Firestone and husband,
Jim, enjoying Power Island, 1991.

Kathleen Firestone

An Island In Grand Traverse Bay

LAKE MICHIGAN ISLANDS
VOLUME I

by Kathleen Craker Firestone

Lake Michigan Islands Series
Volume I
Published by Michigan Islands Research
Northport, Michigan

COVER BY PHOTAIR

Inside front cover: Portion of 1862 map by
John Farmer

An Island In Grand Traverse Bay

ISBN 0-9625631-1-0

Copyright, 1992
Kathleen Craker Firestone

Design and Production by Judy Albaugh
Typesetting by Nick Hamilton

Printed in the United States of
of America by BookCrafters, Inc.

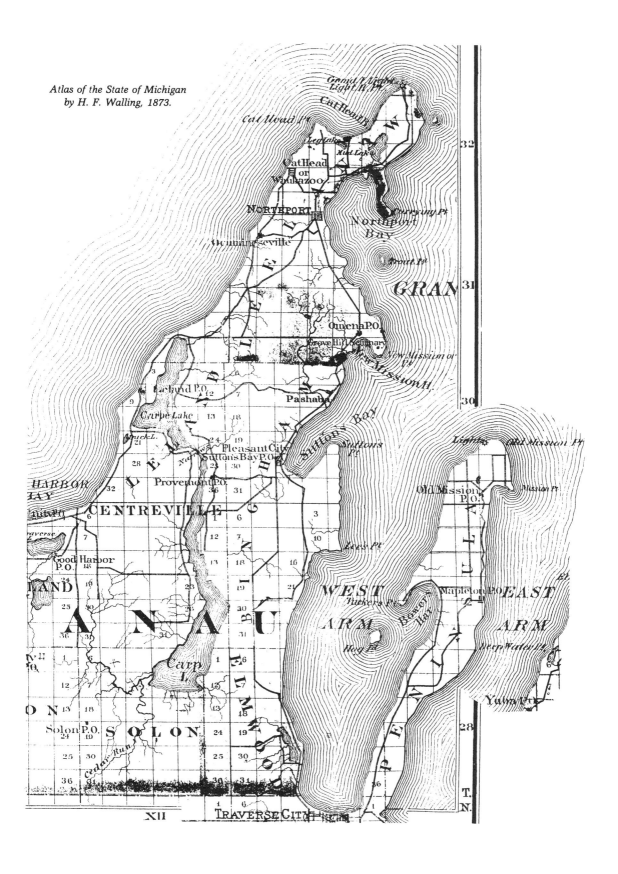

Atlas of the State of Michigan
by H. F. Walling, 1873.

CREDITS

A generous thank you goes to all who helped to make this publication possible.

To those who shared their memories by way of telephone, letter or personal interview: Jim Rennie, Pete Rennie, Jr., John Rennie, A.R. (Bill) Jacobs, Kay Church, Jerome Valade, Margot Power, Willis Pennington, Steve Lockman, Julius Sleder;

To those who played a part in bringing the island into public ownership and who took the time to help me unravel the historical facts of the preservation: Paul Hazelton, Dr. John Spencer, Ted Okerstrom, Eugene Power;

To Dr. Ted Cline for his beautiful aerial photographs and to all who contributed their personal photographs: Elsie Edmondson, John Rennie, Steve Lockman, Paul Hazelton, Margot Power, and others listed elsewhere in these credits;

To the *Traverse City Record-Eagle* for its reporting on the island over the years and for the use of photographs;

To the employees of the Grand Traverse County Register of Deeds Office and County Clerk's Office for assisting in the location of documents.

To Northwestern Michigan College instructor, Fred Tank, for supplying photographs and information and for proofreading portions of the manuscript.

To Jane Norton for photographs and for supplying biological reports on the studies of Dr. William Scharf and June Mason, made for the Nature Conservancy and to Patrick Comer and Gary Reese for survey reports of the Michigan Natural Features Inventory;

To the following libraries and organizations: Northwestern Michigan College in Traverse City, Traverse City Public Library, Institute for Great Lakes Research (Jay Martin) of Bowling Green State University, Henry Ford Archives & Library in Dearborn, Hall-Fowler Memorial Library (Kortne Lampman) in Ionia, the Bentley Historical Library at the University of Michigan, and the State of Michigan Historical Archives (LeRoy Barnett) in Lansing;

To both Steve Harold of the Grand Traverse Pioneer and Historical Society Archives and local historical writer, Larry Wakefield, for supplying information and photographs, for proofreading the historical chapter and for their continued interest throughout the project.

To Nick Hamilton, typesetter, and Judy Albaugh, design and technical engineer of this publication, for their assistance in my historical projects.

To John Pahl, communications instructor at Northwestern Michigan College, who proofread the entire manuscript and offered suggestions.

A special thank you to my husband, Jim, who walked this island's trails with me, assisted in the research of documents, spent many hours working with the photographs and whose interest in local history parallels mine.

TABLE OF CONTENTS

INTRODUCTION

The island has been known by many names since settlers first came to the Grand Traverse Bay area. *Harbor Island, Hog Island, Eagle Island, Marion, Ford, Rennie* or *Power Island,* take your pick. And sometimes part of this 198-acre land mass in Grand Traverse Bay is connected by a tiny islet to a smaller, approximately two-acre island, which has been called *Squaw Island, The Haunted Island, Fisherman's Island,* "but most of all, *Bassett Island.* When Orange Risdon made the land survey in 1852, he included them in one report, simply titled "An Island in Grand Traverse Bay."[1]

Associating it with the islands of Lake Michigan, Marion Morse Davis, in *A Romantic Chain of Islands,* says of this island, "It is as if it were a tiny link dropped from the chain into the bay; or as though there had been three Little Foxes, and the smallest one had run away from his brothers and hid from sight around the Leelanau Peninsula."[2]

Located in the west arm of Grand Traverse Bay, this oasis of beaches and woodlands deserves its rightful place in the recorded history of Northern Michigan and the Grand Traverse area. Being about one mile long and nearly three miles around its perimeter, its shape resembles a diamond; and its natural features include both sandy and rocky beaches and a diverse forest where small woodland creatures live. The Lake Algonquin and Lake Nipissing ages are evident in the benched terrain. The soils are mixed, the dominate soil being of Emmet-Leelanau Association, or in the language of farmers and foresters, "good for growing." The island is easily accessed by a deep-water harbor on the eastern shore.

Being in view from the southwestern shore of Grand Traverse County's Old Mission Peninsula and the southeastern shore of the Leelanau Peninsula, as well as from the beaches of Traverse City at the foot of the bay, the island has long been both a curiosity and an attraction to the mainlander. Now a public parkland, its rich history and its legends add to the value of this "Island in Grand Traverse Bay."

[1] Orange Risdon, Michigan Survey document No. 1290, dated 1852.

[2] George N. Fuller, ed., *Island Stories* (Lansing: State Printers, 1947), p. 363; collection of Marion M. Davis articles from *Michigan History Magazine.*

PHOTO BY J. FIRESTONE

PHOTO BY J. FIRESTONE

FROM PIONEER
TO PRESERVATION

The white man's early explorations of what is now known as the *Grand Traverse Region* were almost exclusively made by the natural waterways. Two French *voyageurs* with the exploration party of Pere Jacques Marquette were Jacques Largillier and Pierre Porteret. In late May, 1673, the two made their way by canoe over "a great crossing," which in French was *la grande traverse.*[1] It was the white man's maiden voyage across this entrance to the beautiful, long bay which connected with "Lac Michigan."

By 1741 Ottawa Indians were moving down from northern camps to the *grande traverse* country, as reported in Ruth Craker's *The First Protestant Mission In The Grand Traverse Region,* originally published in 1932.[2] Craker also wrote that Wasegendaba had been the first Indian settler of the Grand Traverse country, where he at one time lived on the island in the bay.[3] Chief Andrew Blackbird, Indian historian of the 1800's, recorded that the peninsula situated east of the island had been settled by the Ottawas but was turned over to the Chippewas to settle a dispute between the two Indian nations.[4]

Henry Schoolcraft, the Federal Indian Agent, first visited Grand Traverse Bay in 1837, having come down from Sault Sainte Marie. He made his way in a Mackinaw boat, searching for just the right place to establish an Indian mission. What was later to be known as *Bower's Harbor* was considered, as was the little island lying less than a mile out into the bay.

Two years later, in 1839, the Reverends Peter Dougherty and John Flemming arrived and did establish a mission for a camp of Chippewas, around the tip of the peninsula to its eastern shore, out of sight of the Grand Traverse Bay island. The new location came to be called *Mission Harbor* and, later, the peninsula itself *Old Mission Peninsula.* Dougherty wrote in his diary, "I am delighted with the scenery, with the fish, with the limpid waters of the lake, that surpass anything that I have ever seen."[5]

In 1847 Captain Harry Boardman and his son Horace arrived in Grand Traverse Bay aboard their vessel, *Lady of the Lake.* At the foot of the beautiful west arm of the bay, they explored the river Schoolcraft had called the *Ottoway River,*[6] the river that would soon be known as the *Boardman.* They put up a sawmill along one of the tributaries, and Traverse City had its beginning. The Old Mission settlement also increased and by 1851 had about 500 Indians and several families of European origin. In that year the schooner *Venus* brought Perry Hannah, Tracy Lay and James Morgan to the settlement near the Boardman mill, and the schooner *Madeline* arrived to spend the winter at Bower's Harbor, west of the island in the bay. The peninsula, the island and the mainland some seven miles to the south had been planted with the seeds of the white man's civilization.

*Other sources use the spelling *We-we-gen-deby.*

Island Number 10

By 1850 the island had been designated as *Island No. 10* on the cartographers' maps. Two years later it was surveyed by Orange Risdon, thus making it available for homesteading. Risdon's survey said the island was "handsomely situated for a retired farm."[7]

McKinley Wilson, born in Scotland, came by way of Canada and may have been the first white man to live on the island, in the early 1850's, when he was about forty years old. He cleared land on the eastern side of the island and planted a corn field. Staying for only about two years, he then moved to the nearby peninsula where he and his descendants are recorded for years after.

Frederick Johnson, born in Mexico, came to the Grand Traverse area in 1852, when he was 23 years old. He helped with the government land survey from the foot of the east arm of the bay to a line about five miles to the east. Perhaps it was the survey of the island in the bay, also in 1852, which caused him to live on the island for a short time. Soon after, he established his family on the Old Mission Peninsula and became captain of the steamer *Queen Of The Lakes.*

In these days of early settlement, the newcomer often put up a small dwelling on any vacant land, until just the right place was found for a permanent home. Even Reverend Peter Dougherty's settlement moved from the mission site on the peninsula, across the waters to the west, where he established New Mission in 1852, now known as *Omena.*

James Jesse Strang, the self-proclaimed Mormon King of Beaver Island, had already expanded his island kingdoms to the Fox and Manitou Islands and wrote in 1854 in *Ancient and Modern Michilimackinac,* "There is a beautiful island, large enough for settlement, near the peninsula of Grand Traverse."[8] If Strang was planning to send Mormon families to the little island, his dreams were short-lived; Strang was assassinated by some of the Beaver Island residents in 1856. However, there were a few Mormons who left the Beaver Island community and came to live in the Bower's Harbor area to the west of Island Number 10.

Eagle Island — Hawk Island

To many of the early settlers of the Grand Traverse Region, the island in the bay was known as *Eagle Island* or *Hawk Island.* The American Bald Eagle nested there for as many years as the early pioneers could recall. Great numbers of crows also used this land at times for resting places on their travels to points north and south. Perhaps the corn fields of McKinley Wilson provided food for the migrating crows.

Harbor Island — Hog Island

In the early 1860's the island was designated by the United States Government as *Harbor Island.*[9] Some of the locals called it *Hog Island,* and some maps of the mid-sixties titled it that way, even though *Harbor Island* was still its official name. A variation was *Hog's Back Island,* referring to the high rise of the island's silhouette toward the northern end.

The less-seemly title came from the fact that mainland hogs were, in some years, taken to the island in the spring and left to run wild and fatten themselves on the wild berries and the abundance of acorns and beechnuts found on the woodland floor. Some accounts say it was the Ottawa Indians who took their hogs to the island. Others say the white man owned the hogs and stopped the practice of leaving them on the island because the Indians were helping themselves to the animals.

Indians are known to have camped on the island in early years. There are many reports of a salt spring from which the Indians dipped salt water to evaporate down to crystals for cooking and preserving food. Whether they used it to make salt pork, we do not know.

On July 18, 1862, when Archibald Buttars and Daniel C. Benton registered 1812 Bounty Warrants in Grand Traverse County, their property descriptions listed only the sectional parcels. No island name was stated.

Buttars claimed about 138 acres, roughly the eastern half of the island and the northern part of the western side. The rest of the western side and also the southern tip, totaling about 60 acres, were claimed by Benton.

Archibald Buttars was about 26 years old at this time, and apparently had some sort of deal with the new Traverse City real estate team, Bacon & Goodrich, whereby Buttars would gain title to the land and then sell it to the realtors. Buttars was eligible for property from the United States Government through the 1812 Warrant entitlement, "Granting Bounty Land to certain Officers and Soldiers who have been engaged in the Military Service of the United States."[10] Buttars and his young friend, William Wallace Smith, about 14 years old, sailed to the island in the

William W. Smith in later years.

William W. Smith was born in New York in 1849 and came to Traverse City in 1860, when he was just over ten years old, two years after his father died. Smith became a cabin boy in one of Hannah, Lay & Company's steamers at age 14, after first working in a sawmill. Although he did not attend school after age 13, Smith had a "studious turn of mind" and later served as clerk of the steamers *City of Traverse City* and *T. S. Faxton,* as well as in other capacities for Hannah, Lay. He also served the City of Traverse City as mayor and water commissioner.

Grand Traverse and Leelanaw Counties,
pp. 874-875

bay in a wood scow loaded with boards and shingles and built a simple dwelling. After a few days residency, they returned to Traverse City and announced to Bacon & Goodrich that the property was secured.

It seems that Daniel Benton had the same type of agreement with the real estate company. He also gained his property by the 1812 Warrant provision, taking possession of his island property in July of 1862. He and his wife Mary sold it to Albert W. Bacon a month later, for a price of $100. Though the island had the official name of *Harbor Island,* it was referred to on the deed only as "the island near Bowers Harbor."[11]

Archibald Buttars made a little more profit from his larger acreage on the island when he sold it to Bacon in 1864, for $175.

Hannah Lay and Company, with its many business operations in Traverse City, for decades played a major part in the development of the Grand Traverse area. The company ran excursions to Harbor Island with its small steamer *Sunny Side,* beginning 1865. In addition, the *Sunny Side,* with Captain Emery at the wheel, ran regular routes from Traverse City to Elk Rapids, Antrim City, Pine River, Old Mission, Bower's Harbor and Suttons Bay. Frederick Johnson, former resident of the island, was employed by Hannah-Lay to help run the small steamer. In November, 1867, the *Sunny Side* was totally wrecked at Pine River.

John W. Bacon was party to the inheritance of Albert Bacon, and John and his wife Harriet, along with Hattie Bacon, all of Addison County, Vermont, quit claimed this property "known as the Island in West Bay" to Walter C. Bacon on April 19, 1865.[12]

Walter and Georgia Bacon lived in Minnesota and in 1872 sold "all of Hog Island" to William B. Thomas.[13] Thomas was a land speculator from Ionia County, Michigan. In this instance his speculation was secured for a price of $3,000.

The railroad came to Traverse City about that same time, greatly increasing the popularity of the area as a summer resort. The Old Mission Peninsula boasted several cottages belonging to summer folks from the downstate cities. The Neahtawanta Association, based in Ohio, had a large tract of land with a hotel at the point extending into the west bay, about one-half mile north of Harbor Island. The steamers *Crescent* and *Columbia* carried passengers up and down the bay, sometimes taking excursions to Thomas' island property. Land values were increasing and Thomas was soon ready to sell his nearly 200-acre island.

William Thomas and his wife Cordelia did make a sale of the island to Frederick Hall in 1872, for a price of $1,500. Apparently, some other dealing was involved in this sale, since Thomas sold the island for half the price he had paid for it just a few months earlier. Frederick Hall was about fifty years old at the time and was a prominent and wealthy citizen of Ionia. The island was purchased to become part of the inheritance Hall and his wife Ann would pass on to their only child, Marion.

About five years after the purchase, flaws were found in some of the property transfers. In order to correct these, in 1872 Frederick Hall transferred half of his interest to his wife Ann, perhaps for safe keeping, at a price of $3,000. Walter Bacon, son of earlier owner Albert Bacon, quit claimed all of the island to William Thomas, in order to clear up any supposed inheritance from the elder Bacon to his son. It was found that 1812 Warrants had been given on the same property to both Daniel Benton and Noah Bailey. Bailey's widow had inherited from him, but in the end,

Frederick Lewis Johnson was born in Matamoras, Mexico, August 15, 1829. At age 17 he joined the American Navy, was transferred to the land forces under General Zachary Taylor, and served as an interpreter. He was mustered out at Fort Jackson, Mississippi, September 7, 1848. He married Susanna Lowther on Christmas Day, 1855. They lived in Peninsula Township and had ten children.

Grand Traverse and Leelanaw Counties,
pp. 764-765.

Daniel Benton and his wife Mary were recorded as property owners on the east side of the Old Mission Peninsula in 1860.

Grand Traverse County Deeds
Liber 3, p. 360.

Archibald Buttars was recorded as the elected clerk of Leelanau County for the year 1866.

Grand Traverse and Leelanaw Counties,
p. 340

Buttars was born in Manchester, England, November 21, 1838. He moved to Cincinnati with his parents, David and Esther Buttars, and then to Huron County, Michigan, in 1853. Buttars was later president of the Charlevoix County Bank. He worked with lumbering interests in Traverse City and Charlevoix.

"Personal Sketches for Charlevoix County,"
in *Historic Michigan,* p. 412

Buttars died June 5, 1926, in San Diego, California, at age 88. He had been a speculator of pine forests.

"A Romantic Chain of Islands"
in *Island Stories,* p. 363.

Rueben Goodrich served the appointment of receiver in the sale of public lands in the Traverse City District at times during the 1860's and 1870's.

The Traverse Region, 1884, p. 27.

He was born in New York in 1819, moved to Genesee County, Michigan, in 1836 and operated a flour mill, opened a bank and served in the State Legislature. In 1860 Goodrich moved to Traverse City, speculating in land and being active in politics and education.

Grand Traverse and Leelanaw Counties,
pp. 324-326.

Albert Bacon bought property on the Old Mission Peninsula in 1856.

Grand Traverse County Deeds,
Liber 1, p. 561.

Bacon was later recorded living in Elk Rapids, Michigan.

Grand Traverse County Deeds,
Liber 3, p. 161.

Bacon's wife Harriet died in California in January, 1917.

*Thirty-Sixth Annual Meeting and Picnic
minutes of Old Settlers' Association*
June 27, 1917

18

Frederick Hall was born in Vermont in 1816; worked in several land offices in Michigan; was associated with John Ball of Grand Rapids in land speculation; in 1840 was Justice of the Peace in Lyons Township, Ionia County; in 1849 elected to Michigan State Legislature; in 1873 became the first mayor of Ionia; was director of the Ionia and Lansing Railroad and president of the First National Bank of Ionia; married Ann Eager in 1849. Frederick Hall died in 1883 and Ann Hall in 1897. Their family home became the Hall-Fowler Memorial Library in Ionia, Michigan. Documents supplied by Hall-Fowler Memorial Library

Frederick Hall

Ann Eager Hall

Daniel Benton was declared the successor in 1866, four years after Benton had already sold the property to Albert Bacon. This property was also covered in the quit claim from Albert Bacon's son Daniel to William Thomas. All of these corrective procedures made the Thomas deeds clear, and he warranted to Ann Hall the island which he had sold to her husband five years earlier. When all was in order, Ann Hall warranted the property back to her husband Frederick, for the sum of $3,000.

It is not too hard to understand why Marion Hall's parents didn't like their new-found oasis being called *Hog Island,* as it often was. *Harbor Island, Hog Island* — neither suited them. Frederick Hall soon changed the name of his property from *Harbor Island* to *Marion Island,* a change which will soon be explained in further detail. First, the happenings on the adjoining "little island" need to be explored.

Bassett Island — Fishermans' Island

Depending on high or low water, the smaller island contains from two to three acres. When the lake level is high enough, the land is truly an island, surrounded by water on all sides. When the level is lower, the little island becomes a peninsula attached to the bigger island. This sometimes causes confusion because, traditionally, both have separate names, though, legally, they have usually shared a single name.

After being called *Squaw Island* and *The Haunted Island,* the little island became known as *Bassett Island.* The name is a legacy from its first documented white owner, Richard Bassett.

In *Along Traverse Shores,* published in 1891, M. E. C. Bates and M. K. Buck have written in novel-like form about the day they were aboard a yacht which tied up to Dick Bassett's dock on the little island. According to Bate's and Buck's narration, "Him (Dick) and his father used to cross the plains, trading with the Injuns when he wa'n't nothin' but a boy. Then, when the (Civil) war broke out he went into the army, an' take it all around he's got thet peculiar that he'd a good deal rather live all alone."[14] Other accounts also say that Bassett was a Civil War veteran. Exactly when he chose to live on the smallest Grand Traverse Bay island is not clear. Some accounts say he arrived about 1885, but he could also have appeared directly after the war. There were no previous legal property owners of his little island. It seems inconceivable that when all the property of the bigger island had been snatched up in 1862 by Archibald Buttars and Daniel Benton, they would not have staked a claim to the smaller island too, since it was only a puddle-jump away. In addition, neither William Thomas, in the late 1860's, nor Fredrick Hall, in 1872, made any claim to the smaller island, when they each had held all of the bigger island property. A possible explanation may be that someone already had possession of the smaller island by "squatter's rights." Bassett may have taken up residence on the tiny island as early as the 1860's.

Bassett liked solitude. Grand Traverse County had grown to a population of 8,422 by 1880, and the two-plus acre retreat from civilization suited Dick Bassett just fine. Admittedly a hermit, he first built a lean-to shelter on the little island until he could erect a more suitable clap-board home. Bates and Buck described Bassett's house as a "snug little room papered with *Harper's Weeklies,* pictured side out, and half filled by a huge stove."[15]

COURTESY GRAND TRAVERSE AREA PIONEER AND HISTORICAL SOCIETY
Dick Bassett's island hemitage.

Adding a few, small outbuildings and his own private dock, he was prepared for the life of a fisherman. He made friends with some of the local Indians, including Pete Shenango, who loved to share the legends as portrayed in the next chapter. Sometimes the mainlanders called Bassett's little retreat *Fisherman's Island.*

Over the years, Dick Bassett added to the fresh fish on his dinner plate the vegetables and grapes from his island garden and apples from the trees he had planted behind his small house. Bates and Buck's account says of the Bassett garden, "The lack of method or even order, would drive a gardener to distraction, but all things seem to thrive."[16]

Known as a quiet man, Bassett generally kept to himself. He did occasionally have company. Frank Buchan from the Old Mission Peninsula stayed on the island and fished with Dick Bassett from the year 1885, when Buchan was about 15 years old, until sometime in 1887.

Added to human company was the presence of the eagles. Bassett named the female bird "Old Hell Cat" and the male "Poor Him," saying the female reminded him of a woman he had almost married. As quoted in a 1928 story by Nynetta Kroupa of the Old Mission Peninsula, Bassett said of the eagle, "She is the orneriest, cussedest, tormentedest, bossiest female I about ever saw. She don't give that male of hers no peace at all and every time I look at her I think of what I escaped."[17]

In "A Romantic Chain of Islands" written by Marion Morse Davis as part of a series for *Michigan History Magazine* during the summers of 1926-27-28, Davis states that the pair of eagles preyed upon ducks where the Boardman River empties into Grand Traverse Bay, until one was shot and the other never again appeared.[18]

Dick Bassett was a rather private man and was greatly agitated when a Grand Rapids publication, *The Michigan Tradesman*, asked Bassett to write an article about his life, as a follow-up story to one which had been written about him previously.

On October 2, 1985, he penned,[19]

> *About three years ago you wrote me up in The Tradesman. You, of course, thought it would make me feel proud to see my name in print, but I was not proud; far from it, for I partly foresaw the storm that was coming, but I underestimated the severity of the gale. I refer to the newspaper storm that followed your short sketch. That sketch was taken up and strewn broadcast over the land by the newspapers. As it went it gained in quantity and in like ratio, was reduced in quality. I was made to appear as an illicit distiller of whiskey, also as a manufacturer of counterfeit money, and many hints of worse things were thrown out. Result — many people came here to stare at me, ask me numerous absurd and impudent questions; and, at last, one detective came, and, after thoroughly cross-examining me, made a minute search of my house and walked around my island and went through places where he actually had to crawl on his hands and knees. If I had served him right—and done myself justice—I would have doused him.*
>
> *Besides all this, I got letters from all over the land—some decent, some foolish and some abusive; but for some time the papers and people have been giving me a rest, and I had concluded that their anxiety over me had died out. Now, in the name of goodness, why is it that you wish to again tear this old sore open? What have I done that you should single me out to torment, torture and persecute?*
>
> *Last August I went back to Iowa on a visit to my old army friends, and I will state that I was not arrested for murder or any other bad act. One of my old comrades, who has known me for some thirty odd years came home with me and stayed on my island over a month. He was thoroughly pumped by some of the inquisitive people of this region about my past life; but, bless the silly things, they didn't found out anything bad — consequently, they're not happy.*
>
> *For forty years, I have lived quite an active life, and just at present I haven't the time, inclination or paper sufficient to admit of my writing a history of my life— my hands are too sore and I have too much to do; and much as I regret to disappoint you, if you get a 'Life of Dick Bassett, Told by Himself,' you will have to write it, for I will not undertake such a job at present. If it is positively necessary that you print my picture in your paper, do so; and I would suggest that you publish the following lines below it:*
>
> > *"The above is a perfect picture, drawn by our own artist, of Old Dick, the Hermit. It is suspected that he is, or has been, closely connected with all the train robberies that have been committed, during the past five years, in Washington, Idaho, Texas and New Mexico."*
>
> *You had better not put in any safe blowing or bank roberies or murders — leave something to the dear people's imagination, and for the other papers to work on.*
>
> *Mr. Stowe, suppose I should come into your place of business and say: "Here, Stowe, you drop all business now and write me your life history. Now, get it out quick. It won't take any more than a year, and if you don't write it, I will: And I may write something that won't be acceptable to you. You can't help yourself, for I am an editor, and you know by experience that editors don't always get things straight." What would you do: Kick me into the street, of course, and as soon as I could gather my*

scattered senses, I would go away thinking you had done right.
  I gave Miss Cady permission to print my picture, but there was nothing said about the sketch of my life. I think that when one is dead, it is time enough to write the biography. I object to any more newspaper notoriety. Give me a rest and abuse some of these fellows who are running for congress. They like it — I don't.
                                                                              Dick

The locals who were curious about Dick Bassett, but who didn't want to trouble themselves traveling to the island to observe him, could easily find him in winter as he operated a fish market from a small building adjoining the drugstore of P. W. Kane on Traverse City's South Union Street. A group of about ten fishermen brought several kinds of fish to Bassett's market, from the Bower's Harbor area and the waters along the west shore of the Old Mission Peninsula.

In October of 1899 the *Grand Traverse Herald* printed that rumors of a sale of Bassett's island to the Chicago Yacht Club were being denied by Mr. Bassett. Bassett said there was no truth to the reports of a sale and that "when the business is transacted, he hopes to hear from it definitely, as he considers himself an interested party."[20]

In fact, Dick Bassett had been agreeable to the sale of his island, but since he had never officially registered a claim to the property during all the years he had lived there, he did not have legal title. Although he may have been somewhat of a rebel, he quickly saw the need for compliance. Because he had made improvements to the island property by way of the structures he had built, and because he had established himself as a *squatter* he applied for a government patent and was issued it March 27, 1901.

Realizing that his quiet years on the island were over, Dick Bassett moved to Marquette, Michigan, that year, and in December sold his island, his hermitage, to Charles W. Thorne of Chicago, at a price of $2,000.

Apparently, Bassett didn't stay in Marquette for long. In 1906, the local Traverse City newspaper, the *Evening Record,* reported Dick Bassett as "finally getting married, spoiling his reputation as a hermit and disappearing from local gaze." Bassett was said to have moved to California, "somewhere in the Los Angeles area."[21] Bassett did have friends in Los Angeles, Irving and Ellen Newberry, who, in 1898, had given Bassett Power of Attorney to sell their Grand Traverse County property. Perhaps it was the Newberrys who convinced Bassett to join them in Los Angeles. Where he ended up is really not clear. Some accounts say he went to Puget Sound to fish—others, that he returned to his native state of Iowa.

When Charles Thorne bought little Bassett Island, it was with the intent of having a base for a national regatta. The plan was to also purchase the bigger island, which by this time was known as *Marion Island.* The second purchase did not take place, and Bassett Island was not large enough by itself to serve the purposes of the Chicago Yacht Club.

Charles Thorne agreed to sell Bassett Island to the newly-formed Traverse Bay Transportation Company. In the spring of 1906, news spread quickly that a dance pavilion was to be built on the site where Dick Bassett's hermitage had stood for so many years.

Still a Sphinx.

Sketch of Dick Bassett as featured in The Michigan Tradesman, 1882.

On the bigger island, the sound of axe and saw could be heard. Old hemlock trees were marked for cutting. At the same time, hammers began pounding, constructing "progress" on the smaller island.

The dance pavilion on Bassett Island began to take shape. Captain Charles Webb, of the transportation company, lived less than a mile away, on Neahtawanta Point. He worked quickly in the spring of 1906 to get the tourist attraction ready for the summer season. A new 250-foot dock was built to replace Dick Bassett's old fishing dock. The hermit of the island was to be only a memory, and it seemed that even the Bassett name would disappear, evidenced by the fact that the end of the new dock welcomed visitors with a wooden pole trellis which spelled out the name *Marion Island.* Even though ownership of the two islands was still separate, they were now included in one name. Most likely, the water level of the bay was low during that time, merging the two islands into one, as happens from time to time.

The 50 by 100-foot pavilion was a two-story construction, with the dance floor above and the dining room and kitchen below. Electricity was provided by the steamer *Columbia's* dynamo, the *Columbia* being tied to the nearby dock. All was put into operation for the official opening on June 24, 1906.

The first manager of the resort was Jesse Tallerday of Cassopolis, a captain of the *Columbia.* Fred McDonald and Kent Buttars were later hired to manage the attrac-

Marion Island, Traverse City, Mich.

No. 39 Publ. by Orson W. Peck, Traverse City, Mich.

COURTESY GRAND TRAVERSE AREA PIONEER AND HISTORICAL SOCIETY
Marion Island sign welcomes visitors to Bassett Island.

tion and were known as "Robinson Crusoe and his man Friday." Even though the pavilion was constructed and put into use, final sale of the property was not completed until August, 1907, when it passed from Charles and Belle Thorn to Traverse Bay Transportation Company.

The resort attraction gave many hours of fun and relaxation to its visitors. Sunday School groups, high school students, lodges and societies held picnics and other outings on the small island's grounds, taking shelter in the pavilion from sudden rains. The management made every effort to insure that "no improper characters" be allowed, "desiring only a good class of patronage."[22] Dances lasting about two hours each evening were accompanied by area musicians. The recent invention of moving pictures also brought entertainment to the island.

The Traverse Bay Transportation Company, with its line of steamers, carried afternoon picnickers and evening dance partners back and forth between Traverse City and the island, a distance of about seven miles one way. Other trips were made between the island and Bower's Harbor. The *Columbia* and the *Chequamegon*, with their open decks, were the pride of the bay, the larger *Chequamegon* carrying as many as 500 passengers. A ticket on either boat cost twenty-five cents and covered

Visitors come to Bassett Island's dance pavilion.

travel to the island and admittance to the pavilion. The trips were most enjoyable, as recorded in the *Evening Record.*[23]

> After the heat of yesterday, a large crowd took the steamer *Columbia* to Bassett's Island last evening and enjoyed one of the most delightful trips of the season. It looked as if a storm was coming up early in the evening, but the moon came out, the clouds broke and a little breeze blew down the bay just strong enough to keep the pavilion from becoming too warm for the dancers. The island presented a beautiful appearance with the lights peeping from among the trees and throwing their narrow

reflections away across the water while the moon brought out the lights and shadows with beautiful effect. The boat arrived in the city at 11, but it was far too early for the pleasure seekers who vow that every trip is better than the preceding one.

In spite of the enjoyment of the patronage and the good efforts of Captain Webb, the island resort was not very profitable and survived only a few seasons. Its demise was attributed, in part, to the arrival of the automobile to the Grand Traverse area. The new mobility brought opportunities for exploration of other attractions on the mainland.

Advertisements in the Evening Record, July, 1907.

Marion Island

In 1872 Frederick Hall and his wife Ann Eager Hall, of Ionia, Michigan, had purchased the property of William Thomas, the entire acreage of the bigger island. Since it was to be a gift to their daughter Marion, and since the Halls didn't like the unofficial but often used name of *Hog Island,* the island's name was officially changed and sanctioned by the Michigan State Legislature in 1881, from *Harbor Island* to *Marion Island,* much to the consternation of the *Grand Traverse Herald* editor, Thomas Bates. On February 24 Bates wrote,[24]

> *Hog or Harbor island, eight miles down the bay, has been changed to Marion Isle. Harbor Island was the proper name, but for many years the local name of Hog Island had become attached to it, and the present owner became disgusted with it and concluded to change the name entirely. Hog island it is however to the old settlers around the bays, and Hog island it will remain—the legislature of the state of Michigan to the contrary notwithstanding.*

Marion Hall became owner of the ''big island'' when she was thirty-three years old. Her husband, Major Joshua Fowler, moved many times during his military career, and

Marion Hall Fowler

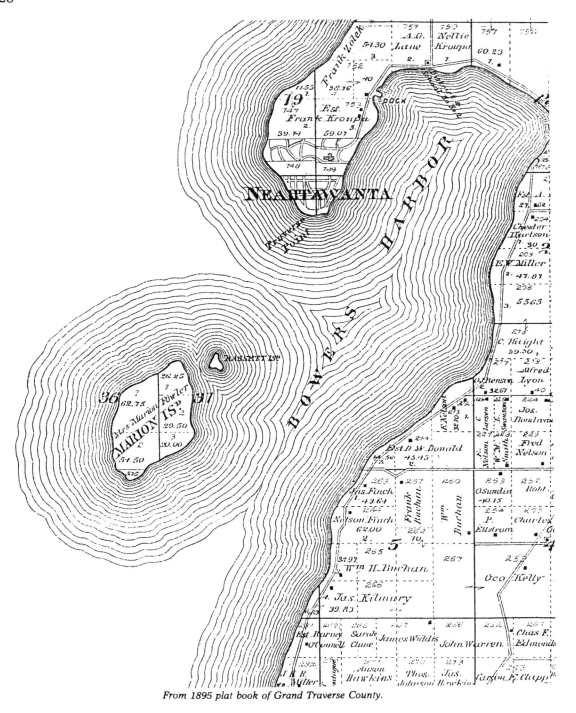

From 1895 plat book of Grand Traverse County.

Marion traveled with him whenever the government allowed. After Major Fowler died in 1898, on his way home from Cuba and the Spanish-American War, Marion Hall Fowler lived in California. From there she found it difficult to oversee her namesake, Marion Island.

The Chicago Yacht Club, which had bought Dick Bassett's island in 1901, had also wanted to buy Marion Fowler's bigger island. Some reports say Charles Thorne, the yacht club agent, couldn't locate Mrs. Fowler. Others say Thorne had made an offer to her, but that she had a bigger offer from someone else. If the yacht club had completed a purchase, plans had been that the two island properties would become a resort with a large hotel, cottages, and docking facilities for big steamers. Whether Thorne never located Marion Fowler or whether she had a bigger offer, no agreement was made between the two. With the bigger island out of reach, the yacht club sold Bassett Island, and the dance pavilion was erected there.

When the pavilion was in operation and many visitors were going to the little island, they also freely used the property of Marion Fowler's big island. It was not unusual for camping parties to pitch their tents and stay for a week or two. Although most visitors were careful, some left camp fires burning, peeled the bark off trees and even cut some of them. Finally at the end of the summer of 1907, Marion Fowler banned picnicking and camping from her property, in order to protect its valuable resources, especially the wide variety of timber. "No trespassing" signs were posted on Marion Island, and it was announced that a fence would be erected between it and the smaller island.

Other signs soon appeared on the island, announcing "This Island For Sale." A. B. Curtis, a Traverse City realtor, was selected by Marion Fowler to oversee the island property and to negotiate a sale. Over the years Mrs. Fowler had received of-

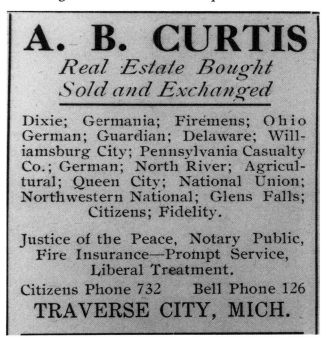

Advertisement from Standard Atlas of Grand Traverse County.

fers to purchase but had been reluctant to sell her property to anyone, this island in the bay, this gift from her parents.

Even after the closing of the dance pavilion on Bassett Island, small groups of picnickers and campers continued to make their way to Bassett and Marion Islands. The steamer *Onekama* was reported in the *Evening Record* to be "doing a good business in the afternoons'' taking visitors to the island, and ''people taking the *Chequamegon*'' back to town.[25]

Hemlock bark was valuable in those days for the tanning of animal skins. Some of the old trees on Marion Island were rumored to be losing their value as a disease threatened to destroy all of the hemlock. It seemed better to harvest them and gain the value of the logs and the bark than to have them die of disease and have no value at all. Whether the reported disease was legitimate remains in question. Perhaps it was; possibly it was merely the advice of some lumberman for harvesting a profitable crop.

Even though the island forest was considered valuable during Marion Fowler's ownership, when scientist Lee Dice of the University of Michigan explored it in 1923, he did not believe the forest to be a very old one. In his 1925 report of the island he wrote, ''Although many of the trees in this forest are of good size, the forest itself is not mature, and the longer-lived trees are far from their maximum growth. It is probable that the present forest is not more than 100 years old; it may not be more than 75 years old. Probably the original forest was destroyed by fire or cutting in the early part of the last century.''[26]

So, according to Dice's observations, the virgin forest of the island had been cut or burned in the early part of the 1800's. Since the Boardmans had erected the first area sawmill in 1847, timber cutting of the island at that time would barely have fallen into Dice's timetable. And why would the early lumbermen travel seven miles to log an island when there was a vast supply of timber all around them on the mainland? If Dice's findings were true to fact, his suggestion that the island's timber may have fallen victim to an early forest fire is probably the correct conclusion. Another possibility may be that a powerful wind storm took down many of the earlier trees. History records occasional destructions on a smaller scale, as winds across the bay have slammed against these acres of ground which rise up out of the waters.

During the hemlock logging of 1909, Birney Morgan operated a livery in Traverse City. Captain Emery's *Fannie Rose* delivered some of Morgan's horses offshore of the island that year, and the horses were forced over the side of the vessel so they would swim to shore. The horses were, most likely, used for skidding the hemlock logs. Charles Allen had been commissioned by Marion Fowler to cut the trees and raft them to a sawmill up the bay on the western mainland shore. When about 500 logs were lost in a storm off Suttons Bay's Lee Point, the steamer *Onekama* was sent to retrieve them. Other trees were cut to open fire lanes around 1910, in order to further protect the island's timber resources.

Though Mrs. Fowler had, just a few years earlier, posted the ''no trespassing'' signs, Hannah, Lay and Company of Traverse City gave out 1,000 free tickets for their annual picnic, held on the island the summer of 1910.

There was much sentiment among the citizens of Traverse City that the island should be in public ownership. Even the First Methodist Church debated the issue, with the question being, ''Resolved, That Traverse City buy Marion Island and convert it into a public park.''[27]

Arguments in favor included that more resorters would come to the area, the boat rides were enjoyable, it would be a cheap means of entertainment for poorer classes of people, and that those confined to the Traverse City area because of their work could travel the short distance to the island and would become healthier and better able to run the city's affairs in later years.

Those arguing against the resolution pointed out the cost of purchasing and maintaining the property, many desirable properties were available within the city, taxes would have to be raised because of other city projects already under way, and that Sunday trips to the island would keep people away from church.

The debate was won by those arguing that the city should not buy the island for a park — and the city did not.

Ford Island

How is it possible for a famous person to buy an island in Grand Traverse Bay, without creating a stir before the transaction is completed? The real estate firm of Nelson and Becker found a way in the spring of 1917. When a promising prospect for the purchase of Marion Fowler's island came forth, the real estate team worked with Traverse City's First National Bank, enlisting the aid of bank employee, Leon F. Titus. On April 21, Titus received a warranty deed from Marion Hall Fowler, for the "sum of One Dollar," conveying "the whole of that certain island in the west arm of Grand Traverse Bay, Grand Traverse County, Michigan, known as *Marion Island . . .*"[28] In subsequent transactions, the Traverse Bay Transportation Company sold Bassett Island to Leon Titus, and Archibald and Emma Buttars quit claimed to Marion Fowler the portion they had sold to Albert Bacon years earlier. On May 16 Leon and Alice Titus completed the "hushed" transaction and warranted Marion and Bassett Island to the new owner.

It was the eighth of June, 1917, and the world was at war, but the *Traverse City Record-Eagle* headlines announced "Henry Ford Buys Marion Island For Summer Home." In smaller print on page two was the report "Ford subscribes for $5,000,000 U.S. Bonds," and the article quoted him, "'To end this terrible struggle we must win. There is no reason why business of America should be alarmed. The war doesn't mean that the wheels of industry will stop or even slow up. The factories will win for us, just as surely as will the men on the firing line.'"[29]

World War I usually was the foremost news of the day, but on this day Henry Ford's purchase of Marion Island rated the first page headlines and outranked even the war news on page two. Ford's words of confidence concerning the war were reflected in his venture in Grand Traverse County. Rumors of grandiose plans for the island spread quickly throughout the region.

The rich folks from Detroit would surely follow the example of their hero and begin buying property in the north, including large tracts of farmland on Old Mission Peninsula. Farmers would have to split their property into smaller tracts so that some could be sold at great profit while others were left for fruit crops. The value of shore property near the island would be in high demand, and the entire Old Mission Peninsula would gradually be converted into a "vast summer colony — one of the largest to be found anywhere."

An electric railway would almost certainly encircle the peninsula, and the outposts of Bower's Harbor and Edgewood would be transformed by "the summer homes of the southern capitalists." Passenger and freight carriers would again be

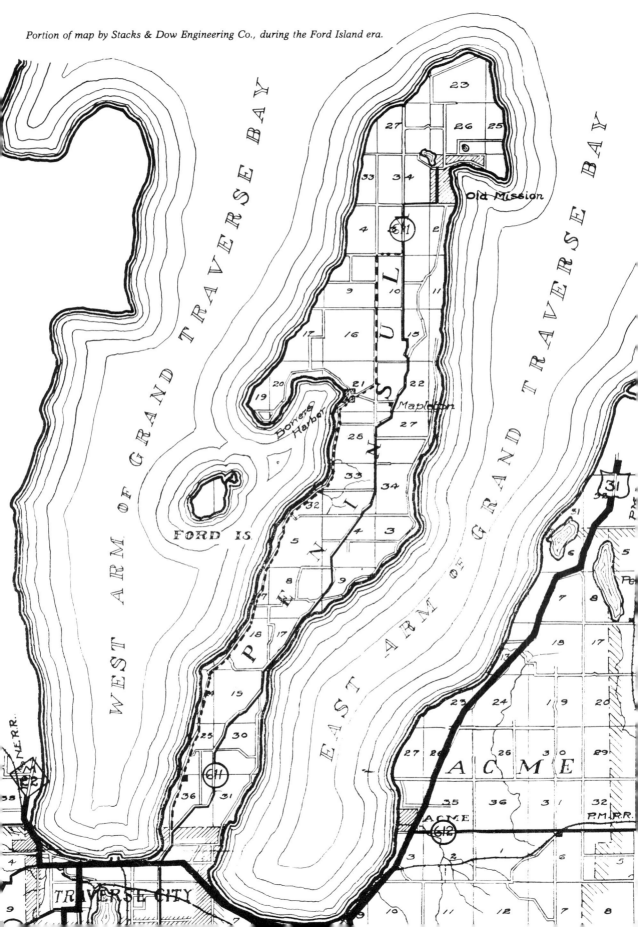

Portion of map by Stacks & Dow Engineering Co., during the Ford Island era.

plentiful on Grand Traverse Bay, and the regattas of years past would certainly be revived.

The *Record-Eagle* ended its report of the purchase with the forecast, "Viewed from any angle, the Ford purchase should bring a stimulation to the resort business of the Grand Traverse Region which will cause it to assume proportions never dreamed of. It will make it the home of middle-west summer people, and when this happens, Traverse City will absorb the reflected social and industrial glory."[30]

With the purchase of Marion Island, Ford also bought the smaller island from the Traverse Bay Transportation Company. For the first time in Michigan's history, the two islands were under one ownership. Together they were to become known as *Ford Island*.

Henry Ford had not previously been on any of the purchased property but had visited nearby Bower's Harbor, which was also the site of the Ford Picnic three years earlier. Proud owners had assembled their new Ford automobiles for this fair-like event. It had been hosted by Milton D. Bryant, owner of the Grand Traverse Auto company and president of the local Chamber of Commerce, who was to become the orchestrator of the purchase of Marion and Bassett Islands by Henry Ford. The fact that Bryant was the brother of Ford's wife Clara may also have played a part in the transaction. In addition to Bower's Harbor, Henry Ford had several times visited Traverse City and had come to appreciate the beauties of the area.

Newspaper accounts told of the expected presence of Ford's yacht sailing the waters of Grand Traverse Bay. That sight was to be delayed, however, because at about the same time the island purchase was announced, Henry Ford released his steam yacht *Sialia* to the United States Navy for service in World War I. He had only purchased the vessel in February of that same year and it had yet to sail the waters of the Great Lakes.

Because Ford still wanted a vessel for his personal use, he bought the gasoline yacht *Widgeon*, which Ford renamed *Sialia II.* In April 1920, when the original *Sialia* was no longer needed for the war effort, Ford bought it back from the government and sold his *Sialia II.*

Ford and his friends and family did visit the island in Grand Traverse Bay, traveling aboard Ford's yacht, which had been restored after the war and was known as "one of the prettiest and most completely equipped private yachts on any water, either fresh or salt."[31] About 200 feet long, it was finished inside and out with rich mahogany, and for safety's sake, held speed boats, swung on davits, one on each side of the yacht. There were five double and four single staterooms, as well as officers' quarters, a saloon, dining room and smoking room. When it was docked at either the Oval Wood Dish dock or the Michigan Transit dock, near other Traverse City business's docks, spectators would line up to get a glimpse of the yacht, and hopefully a peek at its famous owner.

Samuel C. Darrow, the Traverse City property assessor, was employed by Henry Ford to serve as caretaker of the island property. Darrow was knowledgeable about timber; he had operated a saw mill, along with his grocery store, in Bingham Township of Leelanau County. Possibly, it had been his mill where the island's hemlock logs had been sawn just a few years earlier. Darrow cut more fire lanes on Henry Ford's island to help protect the timber resources. During the spring thaws, he sometimes operated a sugar bush on the island, making maple syrup and maple sugar candy from the abundant supply of sugar maples.

PHOTO COURTESY OF THE INSTITUTE FOR GREAT LAKES RESEARCH,
BOWLING GREEN STATE UNIVERSITY *Henry Ford's yacht,* Sialia.

COURTESY KATHRYN CHURCH
*Samuel C. Darrow at about time
he served as island caretaker for
Henry Ford.*

FROM THE COLLECTIONS OF HENRY FORD MUSEUM & GREENFIELD VILLAGE
Crew of the Sialia, *1925.*

FROM THE COLLECTIONS OF HENRY FORD MUSEUM & GREENFIELD VILLAGE
Living Room of Ford's yacht, Sialia, *1925.*

Henry Ford sometimes brought other folks of fame to his island in Grand Traverse Bay. Inventor Thomas A. Edison, as well as Harvey S. Firestone of Firestone Rubber, made short trips to the island, while the wives stayed in comfort at Traverse City's Park Place Hotel. Ford and his friends enhanced the local cultural events. The Detroit Symphonique Ensemble gave a complimentary concert while the Ford yacht was anchored off the Wequetong Club pier, by the Boardman River outlet into Grand Traverse Bay. In a more casual mood, Ford brought Detroit dulcimer player William P. Hallup with him to the Golf and Country Club, where Jep Bisbee played the fiddle at a party in Mr. Ford's honor. The gathering was deemed "one of the most delightful

FROM THE COLLECTIONS OF HENRY FORD MUSEUM & GREENFIELD VILLAGE

Henry Ford (standing) with Mr. and Mrs. Jasper (Jep) Bisbee at Traverse City picnic.

social affairs of the club's season,"[32] with Henry and Clara Ford displaying their talents in dancing the two-step, the Virginia reel and the polka. The Fords also co-hosted dances in the upstairs ballroom of the Grand Traverse Auto building in downtown Traverse City.

The rumors for a big summer resort on Ford Island faded over the years, as well as speculation that the island would become a large game preserve due to Ford's close friendship with naturalist John Burroughs. In the end, about the only thing that changed on the island was the cutting of the fire lanes — that, and the tearing down of the old dance pavilion in 1934. William Foote and Jessie B. Valade, business partners in Grand Traverse Auto, transported the used lumber to Traverse City for other construction projects. Jessie Valade and his son, Jerome, removed all of the hardwood dance floor and reassembled parts of it in their Traverse City home on Spruce Street.

Potential development of the Grand Traverse Bay island was often a subject of conversation on the mainland. Obviously, it would make a unique vacation spot for summer lodges or clusters of cottages. On the other hand, the island was one of the few places in the area that had retained its pioneer, wilderness character. With these opposing goals in mind, William and Grace Foote and A. R. Jacobs made a joint announcement, as recorded in the *Traverse City Record Eagle* on October 11, 1944, that some logging would be done in order to prepare the island for possible future development.[33] In an effort to assure that any development of the island would be done in such a way as to preserve the wilderness flavor, William and Grace Foote completed a purchase of Ford Island from Henry and Clara Ford on October 3, 1944. Eight days later they sold the island to Parts Manufacturing of Traverse City. As had earlier been the agreement between the Footes and A. R. Jacobs, president of the manufacturing company, only the most scientific guidelines would be used for deciding which trees could be removed, without harming the island's beauty and resources. The deed itself stated,[34]

> *Unless essential to a sound forest conservation program, no trees shall ever be cut on said premises by second part, its successors or assigns, which shall at the time of cutting, be less than (12) inches in diameter at the stump, except when necessary in connection with the cutting and removal of larger trees; the building of roads and fire lanes; the creation of gardens parks and recreation areas; the erection of buildings and other improvements, and the essential areas of view in connection therewith.*

A. R. Jacobs was looking for timber which could be used in the World War II effort. His survey of the island revealed a quantity of basswood and fallen timber which could be processed into shipping crates and pallets and transported by boat to Bower's Harbor, where it would be transported by truck to Traverse City. Until that time so little of the island forest had been cut that the tall, forest canopy prevented much sunlight from reaching the woodland floor and, therefore, not much undergrowth was evident. Much of the island had a park-like appearance.

A logging camp was established on the island, and about twenty loggers camped out in tents from May to November in the logging seasons of 1945 and 1946. One attempt was made to boom a large quantity of logs to the western shore of the bay at Greilickville, but this proved to be too expensive and the method was not repeated. Selective

City of Traverse City · Michigan

Commission - Manager Form of Government

January 6, 1961

R E S O L U T I O N

WHEREAS, Ford Island is an aesthetic and recreational asset to
Traverse City and the Grand Traverse area, and

WHEREAS, it has provided a conveniently accessible retreat for the
rapidly increasing number of boating enthusiasts, and

WHEREAS, outside commercial and other interests have been making
concerted efforts to acquire this important property for
private use

NOW, THEREFORE, BE IT RESOLVED that the City Commission hereby
recognize the public service performed by the Rennie Oil
Company by recent acquisition of Ford Island, and

FURTHER, expresses, on behalf of the People of Traverse City, their
sincere thanks, appreciation and gratitude to the Rennie
Oil Company for its announced policy that Ford Island
will continue to be available to the people of this
community for their pleasure and enjoyment as a quasi-
public recreational area.

FOR THE CITY COMMISSION

Hugh R. Murchie
Mayor
Traverse City, Michigan

A Progressive City - - - In the Heart of Michigan's Water Wonderland

logging of the island was directed by the Michigan Department of Conservation, and approximately one million board feet of lumber was harvested over the course of the operations.[35]

Parts Manufacturing Company warranted the island property to F. L. Jacobs Company two years after purchasing it from the Footes. Although preparation of the island for development was announced when Parts Manufacturing purchased the island, no development took place; and the island in Grand Traverse Bay remained a peaceful, green gem to those who passed by its shores.

Rennie Island

In order to settle financial problems, Ford and Bassett Islands were sold in a bankruptcy transaction by F. L. Jacobs to Edward H. Dunn of Kalamazoo, on December 2, 1959. The price was $57.20 in revenue stamps, or $52,000. Mr. Dunn was, in effect, representing Rennie Oil Company of Traverse City, and three days later the property was sold by Edward Dunn to Rennie Oil, a Traverse area gasoline dealer and distributor. Ferris (Pete) Rennie, the company's president, announced that the public was free to visit and picnic on the island during the summer months and that the island would also serve as a wildlife refuge and an arboretum. A Resolution adopted by the City of Traverse City commended the Rennie Oil Company for its action. The Resolution referred to the island as *Ford Island,* some folks still called it *Marion Island,* and now, unofficially, it was *Rennie Island. Rennie* was not a new name in Grand Traverse County; William Rennie first entered Grand Traverse Bay in 1851, when he sailed past the little island in the bay, as part of the crew of timber speculator Perry Hannah.

Now, about 100 years later, Pete Rennie also traveled the waters of Grand Traverse Bay, in his pleasure boat, *Ren's Nest.* At about the time of the island purchase,

The 38-foot trawler, Ren's Nest, *docked at Rennie Island.*   COURTESY PAUL HAZELTON

Ferris J. (Pete) Rennie at the mainland marina.

the Rennie Company also bought Darrow Marina, a watercraft dealership and repair shop located near Traverse City on the western shore of the bay. The business had formerly been owned by Ray Darrow, son of Henry Ford's island caretaker, Samuel C. Darrow. The watercraft business complemented nicely Rennie's island haven. In 1954 Pete Rennie had purchased the 38-foot trawler *Bonnie* and had renamed it *Ren's Nest.* The *Ren's Nest* carried the Rennie family and their many guests not only to Rennie Island, but also to the islands of Beaver and Mackinac and other sites around Grand Traverse Bay and Lake Michigan.

To keep their newly acquired island preserve in order, the Rennie's hired Ralph Matthews as resident caretaker. The island was to be a temporary home for Matthews and his wife Clara; they had been living for the last several years aboard their 42-foot vessel, *Manda,* which was usually tied up along the banks of the Boardman River. Pete Rennie and Ralph Matthews built a cozy caretaker's cabin, complete with stone fireplace, midway up the eastern side of the island. Rennie's sons, Jim and Pete, Jr., often assisted in the island work projects, as well as enjoying the peacefulness of the mariners' retreat. In front of the cabin a crows' nest lookout extended out over the shore line, where approaching watercraft could be easily sighted and welcomed ashore. Ralph Matthews and his wife Clara, who was of Indian descent, were always glad for the visits of the Rennie family. While alone, the

PHOTO BY K. FIRESTONE

The caretaker/ranger's cabin was built by the Rennie family and Ralph Matthews, about 1960, and improved and maintained by their successors.

Matthews' many animals kept them company. Cocoa was their favorite of three monkeys, and another was brought to the island by Pete Rennie as a birthday present for Clara. Added to the menagerie were a number of dogs, and old fox and the

Crow's nest look-out. PHOTO BY K. FIRESTONE

chickens he liked to pester, a big rooster and a noisy parakeet.

Islands attract the adventurous — people like Dick Bassett, people like Ralph Matthews. As recorded by Al Barnes in the *Traverse City Record-Eagle*, Matthews was a skilled mechanic and experienced sailor and had skippered a 38-foot sloop through the Panama Canal and down to the mouth of the Amazon River,[36] as well as the inside passage to Alaska. It had been Matthews' dream to sail around the world and to take Clara outside the State of Michigan, since she had yet to cross its borders. After Mathews bought the decaying sloop *Aquilon,* he had it renamed *Manda* and set to work restoring the vessel. The craft had been given most of Matthews' attention throughout the 1950's. It was in 1960, during the final phases of the restoration, that Ralph and Clara Matthews moved to Rennie Island. But two years later their dream was shattered. While moored for the winter at the Rennie Oil Dock near Traverse City, the *Manda's* hull was crushed by the ice. In spite of all of Ralph Matthews' efforts, the vessel was not seaworthy. It sat for some time in the Boardman River, while Matthews pondered what to do with his broken dream. Finally, the Rennies helped him remove all flotables and chemicals from the *Manda* and towed it just to the south of Rennie Island. There they sent it to the depths of Grand Traverse Bay.

The dream of sailing around the globe was gone, but Ralph Matthews comforted himself by taking care of this little piece of the world, this island in the bay. He developed nature trails, built picnic tables and kept the camping areas in order, built a dock for visitors and kept watch of the great bald eagles that still made their homes in the old tree tops. He also prepared pick-up sites, where the Rennie barge could move close to the island shore to get rocks for the crib of the Sears dock, back on the mainland in Greilickville. He and Pete Rennie could keep in touch by using

Ralph Matthews at the wheel of his dream craft, Manda.   PHOTO BY PHIL BALYEAT

the two-way radio linking the island with the Rennie Oil Company office, close to the Sears dock, just south of Darrow's old marina.

The island was frequented by visitors, both single boat crews and organized parties. The Chamber of Commerce held its annual picnic there, as did the local Coast Guard Auxiliary. Picnickers came for Traverse City's Mayor Exchange Day, the local 4-H club and the boy's softball outings, Traverse City Yacht Club and the Power Squadron gatherings, as well as for other events. Val's dock at Bower's Harbor was often used as the departure point to the island.

Pete Rennie visited the Matthews couple often, bringing supplies and discussing plans for the island refuge. Usually he traveled by way of his *Ren's Nest* or by a smaller boat, except when the bay was frozen. Then his airplane-propeller driven boat-sled transported him across the ice.

On Friday, April 12, 1965, the bay was still frozen. Rennie visited the Matthews

COURTESY GRAND TRAVERSE COUNTY PARKS COMMISSION
Traverse City boy's softball team docks at island for 1961 picnic.

couple that evening and until about two Saturday morning. He arrived home by way of his amphibious sled but decided to make a return trip to the island before noon on Saturday. It was a rainy, foggy day. Radio communications with the island were not clear, and the Rennie family received no confirmation of Pete's arrival on the island. On Sunday the rain was steady and the fog more dense. By Monday the concerns mounted, and Pete Rennie's son Jim heard from a high school classmate that the amphibious sled appeared to be sitting off shore of the island, as the fog lifted. Young Jim contacted his mother, and the two drove along the Old Mission Peninsula's western route, where they, too, sighted the sled.

Pete Rennie hadn't made it to the island that weekend, nor was he to return home. The sheriff's department made a slow journey across the rotting ice, wearing wetsuits and hauling a small, aluminum boat. But all they found were an empty sled and a large crack in the ice. Any footprints had been washed away by the rain. They did find a man's cap and a life jacket. The engine of Rennie's sled would not run at normal power, and speculation was that he tried to walk the rest of the way to Rennie Island or to the mainland but was unable to jump the full width of the crack in the ice. His body was never recovered.

Later that year Rennie Oil Company became a subsidiary of Leonard Oil Company, a downstate firm. The island property remained registered on the county government deeds under the name of Rennie but was controlled by Leonard Oil.

In 1966 Leonard manager, R. Hugh Murchie, advised the local Chamber of Commerce that a private developer from Detroit had offered to buy the island for the price of $120,000. Chamber of Commerce member Paul Hazelton began what was to become a decade-long project of acquiring the island for the public. Within a week of the announcement of the private developer's purchase offer, the Chamber of Commerce made an offer for the same amount. Throughout the ensuing negotiations, Murchie, who had been island owner Pete Rennie's "right hand man," was to

COURTESY GRAND TRAVERSE COUNTY PARKS COMMISSION
Boaters were welcomed to the island by Rennie
and Leonard Oil, 1970.

be a key player in advising the Chamber of Commerce in its pursuit of acquiring the island for the public. Murchie tried to convince President Saboff of Leonard Oil to donate the island to Grand Traverse County instead of selling it; however, this did not come about. Instead, Total Oil Company purchased Leonard Oil and gained control of the island in the bay. The transitional name of *Total-Leonard* was used for the business for a time. Although the island seemed to be out of the public reach, the Chamber of Commerce formed its "Marion Island Committee" that year and set its determined course.

Ralph and Clara Matthews continued as resident caretakers of the island. In November, 1967, they were joined by more residents. Nine yearling deer were transported to the island from the zoo in Traverse City. Doc Aeschliman, the zoo keeper, had raised them for the first year of their lives after they had been orphaned or lost in the mainland woods. But now the zoo's deer pen was overcrowded and the deer too tame to be released on the mainland. The young deer were crated and placed aboard the Rennie barge and taken across the waves to the island in the bay. Matthews lifted the crates with his bulldozer, moved down the ramp and placed the frightened cargo on the land where the deer would be allowed to roam free. For a time the deer sought the company of humans, as they had been accustomed at the city zoo, and would come by the caretaker's area for an occasional petting. Gradually, they adapted to the wild. These whitetails were not the only deer to live on the island; they joined a herd of about thirty. According to Pete Rennie's sons, Jim and Pete, Jr., an earlier barge trip had brought other deer to the island. Also, in 1962, a small herd swam to the island's safety as they were chased by a pack of dogs. Six of those deer remained as Ralph and Clara enticed them with food. Ralph Matthews constructed several elevated platforms about the island, where he could keep tabs on the herd. He and Clara also maintained a year-round supplemental feeding of hay and pellets to the deer.

Ralph and Clara Matthews spent many happy days caring for the island, welcoming

Workmen from Rennie Oil Company and the Traverse City Parks Commission load deer onto the Rennie Barge, 1967. COURTESY TRAVERSE CITY RECORD-EAGLE

Doc Aeschliman (right) of the Traverse City zoo helps unload cargo of deer, with Ralph Matthews looking on. The young deer set out to explore their island home. COURTESY OF TRAVERSE CITY RECORD-EAGLE

COURTESY OF TRAVERSE CITY RECORD-EAGLE   *Clara Matthews welcomes new resident to the island.*

visitors to its shores and aiding sailors in distress. But on a dreary day in September 1970, Matthews took his own life on the island, when he was sick with a terminal disease. Campers who remained after the Labor Day weekend heard the gunshot. Unable to save Matthews, they took his ailing wife Clara to the mainland, away from her island home.

Although some sadness is part of this island's history, it remains, to this day, nearly the same as Pete Rennie and Ralph Matthews preserved it, and much credit should be given to them. Matthews' cabin also remains to serve the needs of other caretakers.

The Lockman family found the door openings a little short at only about five feet, eight inches. Ralph Matthews had suited the building to his own size, but Alan Lockman and his son, Steve, had to dip under the low frames during their four summers at the cottage, after Al Lockman was hired in 1971 by Total-Leonard Oil's manager. Lockman was a teacher at Traverse City's high school and especially enjoyed his work with the Outdoor Education Center program. Students of the program helped in the spring clean-up of the island and enjoyed the experience of camping on an island and observing its biology. Some others taking advantage of the attractions of the island were the Boy Scouts and Girls Scouts, Chamber of Commerce, church organizations and college student groups, as well as many family units.

One of the Lockman's first jobs was to get rid of the animal houses and pens left by Ralph and Clara Matthews. The Lockmans had visited the island while the Matthews

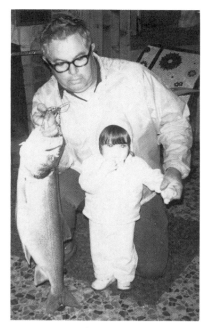

Caretaker Allen Lockman measures a large catch next to granddaughter Stephanie, 1973. Stephanie Lockman enjoys a view from the crow's nest, 1974. *COURTESY STEVE LOCKMAN*

were caretakers but didn't often venture close to the cabin or into the woods because of dogs that sometimes ran loose. A property appraiser hired by the Marion Island Advisory Committee had not included the caretaker buildings in his 1968 appraisal because they "were not a major factor" and because the buildings were "enclosed with a six-foot high fence which is patrolled by at least three large German shepherd dogs."[37] Besides cleaning up the dog houses and animal pens, the Lockman family made repairs to the cabin, maintained the picnic grounds and trails and kept track of the deer herd. A salt block near the cabin was a favorite stop for a large buck. Wild turkeys, which had been planted on the island, came to the back porch as Steve and wife Laura and young daughter Stephanie threw grain to them. According to Steve Lockman, "It sure was a good living out there."[38]

1968 view of caretaker's cabin and outbuildings. PHOTO BY DONALD V. WHIPP, JR.

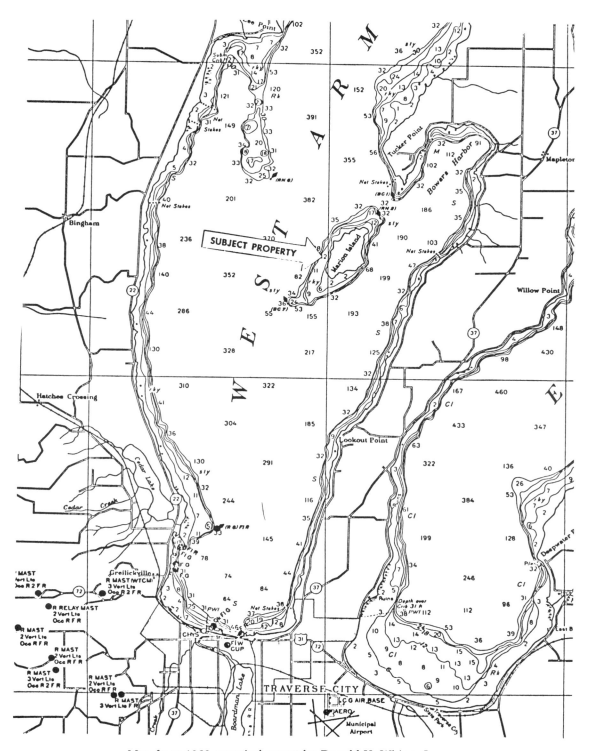

Map from 1968 appraisal report by Donald V. Whipp, Jr.

The public acquisition movement was gaining strength in the Grand Traverse Area among others who also thought it was "good out there." Dr. Frank Power wrote to Conservation Chairman Harry C. Whiteley on March 5, 1968,[39]

> ... *The Federal Government, the State of Michigan, and local municipalities are spending millions of dollars to encourage boating and the utilization of the great natural resource, our Great Lakes. We must not forget, however, that there is more to boating than just dashing from marina to marina before one's ice cubes melt. Many boaters are very anxious that we preserve some relatively unspoiled harbor areas where the less timid, and those who are not so interested in hooking up to 110 current can anchor and fish and enjoy "getting away from it all." Marion Island offers such a place . . .*

The Department of Natural Resources was interested in making the island public property, but the department's interest included bigger and more modern marina and camping facilities on the island. That was not what the local citizens had in mind.

POWER ISLAND

In early 1970 Paul Hazelton, who was a local architect and a member of the Grand Traverse County Board of Commissioners, as well as president of the Traverse City Area Chamber of Commerce, announced that the Chamber had been negotiating to purchase the island in the bay and that it would be "used for public recreational purposes."[40]

Hazelton himself had enjoyed visiting the island many times and had often traveled there aboard the *Ren's Nest,* which he had renamed *Queen Mary* when he purchased the vessel from the Total-Leonard Oil company in 1968, three years after Pete Rennie's disappearance. The Chamber held its annual picnic on the island again that year, and in subsequent seasons, and its members continued their belief that others should also have access to this island treasure.

Throughout the years and the many changes in ownership, the island had escaped residential development. Northern Michigan, and especially the Grand Traverse Area, was on the verge of a development boom as more and more visitors began to realize the unique beauty of the area. The Chamber of Commerce continued its efforts in ensuring that the island with so many names would be preserved in the name of the public. Dr. John Spencer served as Chamber president in 1971, and Ted Okerstrom served the post in 1972.

Working with Total Oil Company, the Chamber of Commerce agreed on a purchase price of $500,000. Because no local funds were available, and because possible development by a private party was threatened, contact was made with the Nature Conservancy, a national, non-profit, environmental agency based in Arlington, Virginia. The Nature Conservancy obtained an option on the island and held it while a search was made for a donor or donors to contribute the needed funds for purchase.

In September of 1973 the Chamber of Commerce's Marion Island Committee chairman, Paul Hazelton, was contacted by an individual who wanted his identity kept secret, even from the other committee members. In response to his own question of "What can I do for Traverse City?" the anonymous person offered substantial funds for a matching grant for the purchase of the island. In 1974 an application was made to the Resources Conservation and Development Program, administered by the U.S. Soil Conservation Service, for the other half of the matching grant. The Grand Traverse County Board of Commissioners also gave approval for the county to accept the island as county property.

Mr. Cannon, Paul Hazelton, Jim Collison, Paul Grindell and Al Brown prepare to travel to island to make Soil Conservation survey of necessary work projects. COURTESY PAUL HAZELTON

After further negotiation, in July, 1975, the donors for the matching grant were finally announced. Eugene and Sadye Power contributed $250,000 to the Nature Conservancy for purchase of the island, along with an additional $21,000 to Grand Traverse County for half the estimated cost of necessary improvements to the park. The island's most significant benefactor, Eugene Power, was born in Traverse City in 1905, and at the time of the island purchase, was owner of the Park Place Hotel. Hotel manager Ted Okerstrom, who had also been Chamber of Commerce President in 1972, had transported the Powers to the island as they were in the process of deciding their role in the island acquisition. Although Eugene Power and his wife were now residents of Ann Arbor, he had spent the first twenty-two years of his life in Traverse City, and as children, he and his brother Frank had made many sailboat trips to the island with their parents. As a teen-ager, Frank had found an abandoned sailboat and restored it, naming it the *Spray.* Eugene and Frank had sailed the *Spray* to the island and had camped there by themselves. In an interview for the *Traverse City Record-Eagle,* Eugene Power said, ''As a youth I fished, swam, sailed, skied and enjoyed this whole country . . . I developed a great affection for the area and its natural resources. Marion Island occupied a special place for me, and later on for Sadye after we were married.'' In another interview Power stated that his ''primary concern was to make certain that the island would be preserved in its present wild state and that it be used by the general public for daytime use.''[41]

Out of the Chamber of Commerce, the Marion Island Corporation was established as a non-profit corporation to preserve and manage the island park. Deed

The local Chamber of Commerce enjoys another picnic on the island, now a public park. COURTESY PAUL HAZELTON

restrictions on the purchase stated:[42]

1. Marion Island shall be preserved in perpetuity as a public wilderness park unspoiled and undeveloped for the use and benefit of the general public.
2. Marion Island shall be managed according to the established principles of good forestry and wildlife management. It shall never be logged and there shall be no cutting of trees, logs or flowers except such as shall be dictated by good forestry and wildlife management.

The first members of the Marion Island Commission, whose duty it was to handle the business of the Marion Island Corporation, were Dr. John Spencer, who served as chairman of the committee and was also County Health Director, past president of the Grand Traverse Area Chamber of Commerce, a local history buff and an environmentalist who had a keen sense of the island's ecological status; Paul Hazelton, who for some ten years had been the driving force in the public acquisition effort; Hugh Murchie, manager of Total-Leonard Oil, and apt negotiator and trouble shooter between the buyer and seller; Dr. Frank Power, strong environmentalist and intermediary between the committee and his brother, island acquisition donor, Eugene Power; John Sabo, local high school teacher who had assisted in the island caretaking; Sondra Shaw, member of the Grand Traverse County Board of

Commissioners; William Wise, whose guidance was indispensable, as attorney for the Chamber of Commerce and for Peninsula Township; and Dr. James Hall, who made many trips to Lansing to negotiate for Federal outdoor recreation funds. One of the committee's first duties, after being appointed in 1976, was to establish guidelines for use of the island park.

Al Lockman had continued as caretaker of the island in 1975, and it was his privilege to welcome visitors to the newly acquired public preserve and to enforce its preservation.

With the island coming into county ownership that year, an immediate problem which had to be resolved was that of the deer. Released on the island in 1959, nine deer had joined about thirty already in residence, and together they had multiplied so much that they were destroying the island's vegetation. Ground hemlock, which had been abundant through the island's forest, had all but disappeared, being a favorite food of the deer herd. Other species of vegetation also suffered the browsing of the whitetails. Private deer hunts by the island's owners had taken place since 1970, although only mature bucks had been removed.

Michigan Department of Natural Resources wildlife biologist Bob Odom recommended that all the deer be eliminated or that only one sex of deer be left, in order to prevent the population from further explosion. The vegetation on which the deer fed was not reproducing as fast as the deer were consuming it. This was not healthy for the whitetails, nor was it wise to allow such destruction of the natural plant life.

The Marion Island Commission concurred; and with the deer population about doubling between 1975 and 1976, the advisory board worked with the DNR toward hunting seasons to remove the deer. By then the ground hemlock was observed to be almost completely browsed out, as were many wild flowers. In 1976, the first public hunting season, approximately 64 deer were taken from the island. Attempts to completely eradicate the deer were difficult, since deer under pressure of a hunt have been known to swim to the mainland, only to return after the season is ended. The second public hunting took place in 1977. No deer were observed by caretaker Jack Clark during the summer of 1978, and the deer are believed to be completely gone now. While the elimination of the deer became a point of argument for some local citizens, biologists generally agree that deer herds within the boundaries of islands are not a good idea, if valuable plant life is to be preserved.

Hired in the 1977 summer season, Jack Clark, a Traverse City High School English teacher and sports coach, found island living to his liking and served as caretaker for that and several years after. More than 3,000 visitors were recorded on the island in 1977, the first year records were kept. Following Clark, another Traverse City High School teacher, Jerry Urban, also served as caretaker.

The island was now securely public property. Visitors would no longer have to ponder the future of this lovely, green diamond in the bay. Paul Hazelton wrote in his *Queen Mary's* log book on July 24, 1978, "To Marion Island—to take a walk and see sunset."[43] Knowing that future generations would be able to follow his path along the shore, could there be any greater reward for his years of effort toward preserving this island for the public?

Other citizens also maintained their interest in this now-public island. John and Jane Norton, residents of Traverse City and members of the state's Nature Conservancy, made yearly volunteer inspections of the natural features of the island during the early 1980's. John Norton was also a member of Grand Traverse County's parks commission, established in 1975. The Nortons were instrumental in obtaining funds and arranging for an ecological inventory of the island, and some of the results of those studies are included elsewhere in this book.

In 1985 Fred Tank, a Northwestern Michigan College science instructor, took over the duties of island caretaker and began the first of many seasons on the island. He and his wife Tina and their six children joined the ranks of family caretakers to watch over and maintain the island park.

COURTESY TRAVERSE CITY RECORD-EAGLE
High water destroyed the island's dock in 1985, shortly after this inspection
by caretaker Fred Tank and resulting in construction of a new dock.

COURTESY TRAVERSE CITY RECORD-EAGLE

Caretaker Fred Tank's family in front of ranger's cabin in 1986. L-R are Tank's nephew, Garrett Tank; children, Jason, David, Alexander and Elizabeth; and wife Tina.

Although the island has been called by many names throughout the years, most have not been officially recognized by the U. S. Government. *Marion Island* was still the official name in 1975, when the island became a public park. In 1986, the Grand Traverse County Board of Commissioners adopted a resolution giving approval for both the large and small islands to be named *Power Island,* in honor of Eugene and Sadye Power, the donors who made the acquisition possible.[44] After the death of Eugene Power, and as United States navigational charts are revised, the charts will reflect the name of *Power Island* for the island in Grand Traverse Bay.

145-86
R E S O L U T I O N

Recognition of Eugene & Sadye Power

WHEREAS, What has long been termed Marion Island has become an outstanding recreational resource for the citizens of the Grand Traverse Area; and,

WHEREAS, Although many people were involved in its acquisition by the County, it was the magnificent generosity of Eugene and Sadye Power that provided the definitive gift allowing this island to become publicly acquired; and,

WHEREAS, An appropriate long last designation of their role is fitting that we should commerate this achievement for the benefit of present and future generations and change the name of Marion Island to Power Island,

NOW, THEREFORE, BE IT RESOLVED BY THIS BOARD OF COMMISSIONERS THAT, In honor of Eugene and Sadye Power's generosity and love for the Grand Traverse Area, Marion Island is hereby officially named Power Island,

Karen B. Stron, Chairman
Grand Traverse County
Board of Commissioners
Dated: November 26, 1986

Chamber of Commerce member, Dr. John Spencer, presents a photograph of Power Island to benefactors, Eugene and Sadye Power, at island's dedication ceremony in 1987. PHOTO BY FRED TANK

POWER ISLAND DEDICATION

Today's ceremony is significant for several reasons, I believe, beyond the evident ones. Certainly this island is beautiful and accessible and provides recreational opportunities along with a storied history — some of which is yet to be discovered.

And it's fitting to designate a new name, Power Island, to recognize in this way the unique contributions of those two individuals who, more than all others, allowed its public acquisition to occur when it did. But beyond this day's ceremony, I believe some fundamentally important concepts need to be perceived.

First, the island's acquisition is an EXAMPLE of what can occur with natural resources when people are willing to work for something beyond themselves—to pursue a commitment consistently and to overcome obstacles. It demonstrates that worthwhile goals can be achieved and that local opportunities require effort locally. It particularly illustrates not only what happened here but what did not. For it would have been easy to give up along the way. Except for leadership, especially Paul Hazelton's leadership, that could have happened. And this island, likely, would now have entirely different signs along its beaches. Fortunately, nowadays this idea of a necessary commitment, a partnership with opportunity, is no longer so rare. Twenty years ago, it was. Even now, it's more often an exercise in optimism than a reality.

Secondly, the preservation of Power Island is a SYMBOL of this area's natural wonder and our heritage; for our legacy of blue waters, bright hills, clean beaches and quiet opportunities. For an access to nature, locally and regionally, that remains enviable but which most of us have done little or nothing to maintain or conserve.

In a quieter sort of way, it's a symbol also of fortuitous circumstance; to the 1879 ownership of Frederick Hall and his daughter Marion and to that of Henry and Clara Bryant Ford beginning in 1917. Between them, the island's present characteristics were preserved for 65 years. In another way, it's a symbol that we need to do more and to do it more effectively, if much of this heritage, now rapidly changing, is to be retained.

For islands are easily seen. They have a clear and special identity and are simple to define. Their margins are geographic. Their boundaries allow specialized management which their limited access facilitates. Further, these characteristics catalyze a singleness of purpose in people and a degree of cooperation not readily transferred.

Thirdly, the redesignation of this island as Power Island serves as a CHALLENGE to our community; to a recognition that we have debts to pay not only to the past but to the future; to the idea that wholesale exploitation of resources has got to stop sometime, somewhere and that the quality of life demands a decent respect for the environment; that development ideally requires a compact with nature and not an extraction from it; that not every hill with a view deserves a homestead or every automobile a new bridge;—and to transpose these concepts to the mainland.

For over there, these views so conveniently segregated here are controversial if not litigious. Because the margins of their implementation are diffuse and their propriety questioned. Admittedly, here in this area we started with more. But that doesn't mean we have less to conserve. So the challenge remains—along with this symbol and this example; how best to utilize and yet conserve. And for this standard we can be grateful; to the island's prior owners and to their ownership; to the leadership of Paul Hazelton and the activity of Pete Rennie; to all the individuals who participated in these efforts; to the Nature Conservancy and the various governments; and to the farsighted philanthrophy of Eugene and Sadye Power. Without them all, we would not have this place. And we would not have such an opportunity to match in other times and in other ways.

John Spencer
September 7, 1987

Eugene Power was born June 5, 1904, and spent the first 22 years of his life in Traverse City. After graduating from the University of Michigan with a masters degree in business, he worked for a short time in Chicago for a construction company and then returned to Ann Arbor to work for the printing firm, Edwards Brothers, Inc. Earning the name "Mr. Microfilm," after inventing and marketing the process for reducing documents to small film strips, Eugene Power also served for ten years on the U. of M. Board of Regents. His local interests include ownership and renovation of the Traverse City landmark, Park Place Hotel, in the 1960's, and procurement of the Eskimo Art Collection for Northwestern Michigan College, while promoting Eskimo art world-wide. After merging University Microfilms with the Xerox Corporation in 1962, Eugene Power retired in 1970, but maintained his home in Ann Arbor, where he his wife Sadye based their family philanthropic foundation.

Sadye Power, a well-known psychiatrist, founded the student mental health service at the University of Michigan.

Sunrise over the island in Grand Traverse Bay, 1991.   PHOTO BY K. FIRESTONE

Thanks to the many pioneers who resisted development and to those who worked to preserve the island for the benefit of the public, this little gem in the bay will remain much as it was when the first white men set foot on it. Special credit goes to Grand Traverse Area Chamber of Commerce Presidents Paul Hazelton, Larry Hardy, David Pearce, John Spencer and Jack Bensley, who pursued the dream of preserving the island for all of us to enjoy and who dedicated themselves to turning that dream into a reality. And, of course, the visitors who frequent Power Island are forever in debt to the donors of the acquisition funds, Eugene and Sadye Power.

Dick Bassett, Marion Hall-Fowler, Henry Ford, Pete Rennie and others would be happy to know that this island in Grand Traverse Bay is being preserved as they knew it. So would Old Mission Peninsula resident Nynetta Kroupa, who wrote in 1928,[45]

> *How often in the morn as I rise from my pillow,*
> *and gaze from my window at the break of day,*
> *I see in the distance a beautiful island,*
> *rising majestically out of the bay.*
>
> *Oh beautiful island, Marion Island,*
> *Island of legends in Grand Traverse Bay,*
> *We love your green verdure, your history's a treasure,*
> *You beautiful island out there in the bay.*

On September 7, 1987, Power Island was officially dedicated and its public acquisition celebrated.

PHOTOS BY FRED TANK

Eugene Power and son Philip inspect the dedication plaque and enjoy visiting with the celebration guests.

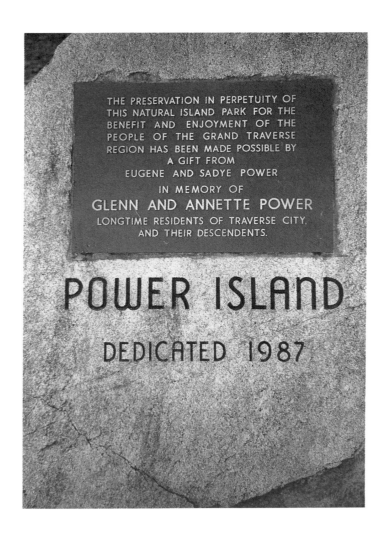

THE PRESERVATION IN PERPETUITY OF
THIS NATURAL ISLAND PARK FOR THE
BENEFIT AND ENJOYMENT OF THE
PEOPLE OF THE GRAND TRAVERSE
REGION HAS BEEN MADE POSSIBLE BY
A GIFT FROM
EUGENE AND SADYE POWER

IN MEMORY OF

GLENN AND ANNETTE POWER
LONGTIME RESIDENTS OF TRAVERSE CITY,
AND THEIR DESCENDENTS.

POWER ISLAND

DEDICATED 1987

Because of the generosity of Eugene and Sadye Power and the efforts of local citizens, Power Island is preserved for the enjoyment of present and future generations.

[1]"First white men cross bay in May, 1675," *Traverse City Record Eagle,* 22 May, 1976, p. 13.

[2]Ruth Craker, *The First Protestant Mission In The Grand Traverse Region* (1935; reprint, Mount Pleasant, MI: Rivercrest House, 1979), p.8.

[3]*Ibid,* p. 58.

[4]Andrew Blackbird, *History of the Ottawa and Chippewa Indians of Michigan* (Ypsilanti, MI: Ypsilanti Job Printing House, 1887), p. 15.

[5]Craker, p. 61.

[6]Henry Schoolcraft, *Narrative Journal of Travels (1820),* ed. Mentor L. Williams (Michigan State College Press, 1953), p. 263.

[7]Michigan Survey Document No. 1290, Orange Risdon, 1858.

[8]James Strang, *Ancient and Modern Michilimackinac* (1854; reprint, Mackinac Island: W. Stewart Woodfill, 1959), p. 87.

[9]J. H. Colton, *Colton's Tourist Map of the Great Lakes* (New York), located at Clarke Historical Library, Central Michigan University, Mount Pleasant, MI.

[10]*Grand Traverse County Record of Deeds,* Liber 18, p. 113.

[11]*Ibid,* Liber 4, pp. 356, 357.

[12]*Ibid,* Liber 5, p. 521.

[13]*Ibid,* Liber 9, p. 507.

[14]Mrs. M. E. C. Bates and Mrs., M. K. Buck, "In a Yacht From Traverse City To Mackinac," in their *Along Traverse Shores* (Traverse City, MI, 1891), p. 195.

[15]*Ibid*

[16]*Ibid*

[17]"Marion Island," unpublished manuscript by Nynetta Kroupa, 1928, in the collection of the Grand Traverse Area Pioneer & Historical Society Archives.

[18]George N. Fuller, ed., *Island Stories* (Lansing: State Printers, 1947), p. 363, collection of Marion M. Davis articles from *Michigan History Magazine.*

[19]"Bassett's Island Has Colorful History," *Traverse City Record Eagle,* 28 Oct., 1959, p. 16, as quoted from *Michigan Tradesman,* 1885.

[20]"Island Is Not Sold, *"Grand Traverse Herald,* 19 Oct., 1899, p. 5.

[21]"Will Erect Big Pavilion," *Evening Record,* 4 May, 1906, p. 3.

[22]*Ibid*

[23]*Evening Record,* 29 June, 1906. P. 1.

[24]*Grand Traverse Herald,* 24 Feb., 1881, p. 3.

[25]"Marion Island News," *Evening Record,* 10 July, 1907.

[26]Robert Hatt, *Island Life* (Bloomfield Hills, MI: Cranbrook Institute of Science, 1948), p. 39.

[27]"Won't Buy The Island," *Evening Record,* 27 March, 1907.

[28]*Grand Traverse County Record of Deeds,* Liber 97, p. 268.

[30]*Ibid*

[31]*Ibid*

[32]"Jep Bisbee Fiddles, As 200 Dance With Fords," *Traverse City Record Eagle* 19 July, 1924, p. 1.

[33]"Ford Island is sold to Parts Mfg. Company," *Traverse City Record Eagle,* 11 Oct., 1944, p. 1.

[34]*Grand Traverse County Record of Deeds,* Liber 495, p. 151.

[35]A. R. Jacobs, letter to author, dated 25 Nov., 1991.

[36]Al Barnes, *Traverse City Record Eagle,* 28 Oct., 1953, p. 1.

[37]Donald V. Whipp, Jr., *Marion Island, West Arm of Grand Traverse Bay,* 1968 property appraisal, pp. 23-24.

64

[38]Steve Lockman, telephone interview by author, December, 1991.

[39]Frank H. Power, M.D., letter to Harry C. Whiteley, dated 5 March, 1968.

[40]*Traverse City Record Eagle,* 11 Feb., 1970, p. 1.

[41]"Power is Island $ Donor," *Traverse City Record Eagle,* 23 July 1975, p. 1.

[42]Grand Traverse County Board of Commissioners, Resolution No. 48-75.

[43]Paul Hazelton in nautical log of yacht *Queen Mary,* 24 July, 1978.

[44]Grand Traverse County Board of Commissioners, Resolution No. 138-86.

[45]Kroupa, un-numbered page.

PHOTO BY K. FIRESTONE

OPPOSITE PAGE: AERIAL BY PHOTAIR

The schooner Malabar, *patterned after windjammers of the mid-1800's, sails the waters of* Grand Traverse Bay *and in front of the bay's island, renewing a scene from the area's past.*   PHOTO BY FRED TANK, 1991

Visitors enjoy Bassett Island and the dance pavilion.　　　　　ELSIE EDMONDSON COLLECTION

Columbia *docked at Bassett Island.*

ALONG THE SHORES OF TRAVERSE BAY.

Photo Copyrighted by Orson W. Peck, Traverse City, Mich.

Marion Island as seen from shores of Old Mission Peninsula.

Paul Hazelton at ship's wheel of his 1938-built pleasure craft, Queen Mary, *formerly Pete Rennie's* Ren's Nest.
COURTESY PAUL HAZELTON

Eugene and Sadye Power pose beside dedication plaque on Power Island in 1987. The island is now preserved for enjoyment by Power's son, Philip, and grandson, Nathan, (pictured) as well as for present and future generations of the general public.   COURTESY MARGOT POWER

PHOTO BY K. FIRESTONE

Bassett Island, The Island of Dread, The Haunted Island.   PHOTO BY FRED TANK

LEGEND AND FANTASY

Intrigue and mystery are often attached to islands. There seems to be something about their character that invites romanticism. Most every island can claim buried treasure, a peculiar hermit, or some other legend, however modest or obscure.

Indian legends in Northern Michigan abound, and there are a few concerning this little refuge in Grand Traverse Bay. One tells of a camp of Indians who first lived on the west side of the ''big island'' but relocated in fear to the east side, after being terrified by a ghost. The ghost, a white man wearing overalls and a shirt with rolled-up sleeves, took the form of a blacksmith. The specter could be seen walking along the shore and dipping water into a pail, but leaving no footprints. The clanging of his blacksmith's hammer throughout the night sent the terrified Indians fleeing to their new eastern camp, never to return to the old site. Variations of this legend exist, with blacksmith still seen and the clang of hammer and anvil still heard, sometimes accompanied by the mooing of cattle in the woods.

We humans are good at story telling. If an island seems to be lacking in mystery, we invent some. Such was the case with this next ''legend.''

''. . . Kensotis was chief of a tribe of Indians that lived on the Peninsula years ago. He was in continual conflict with the northern tribes and each year made sorties into far away Canada on missions of battle and conquest. Fortune favored him and he was in a fair way of controlling all of what is now Northern Michigan, when disaster overtook him.

''A great force of Indians came from across Lake Michigan and landed near what is now Elk Rapids, with the express purpose of overcoming Kensotis, whose fame had spread even to their villages. When the chief heard of the hostile tribe in his territory, he immediately summoned his fighting men and ordered to take their war canoes and go to meet the strange Indians.

''When the fleet was but a short distance from the mainland, a great storm from the north arose and swamped all of the canoes but that of Kensotis and a half dozen of his paddlers. As soon as the storm abated, the hostile Indians captured the great chief and his few men. The latter were made slaves and the chief was exiled to what is now Marion Island. The new tribe took over all of Kensotis' territory and also kept Meahnonta, his beautiful daughter, as a hostage.

''One night Meahnonta fed her guard some of the 'sleeping root' and escaped. Undaunted by the distance, she entered the water near what is now Neahtawanta and swam to her father on the island. The Indians left them undisturbed until a day that Wasebic, son of the chief of the hostile Indians, pursued a wounded deer in his canoe. The deer swam to the island and Wasebic followed. Here he saw for the first time the beautiful Meahnonta.

''Mutual love was instant and Wasebic decided to make the island his home and forsake his tribe. When the word of this reached his father, a war party was organized and started for the island to capture the errant tribal son. Kensotis, Meahnonta and Wasebic stood on the bluff on the south side of the island and watched the approaching party, firm in their determination to fight until overcome or killed.

''As the party reached the shore immediately under the three island dwellers, Wasebic discharged an arrow at the party. In so doing, his foot slipped and dislodged a large stone which started falling toward the war party. As it fell, it loosened other rocks and soon the entire bluff was falling. The father and two lovers

South-side bluff inspired the "legend" of Wasebic and Meahnonta.　　　　PHOTO BY K. FIRESTONE

gained firm ground just as the whole side of the island slipped into the water, carrying the entire war party with it. Every one of the attacking party was drowned and never a body was recovered, but the three Indians spent the remainder of their lives in comfortable solitude.

"The white scar on the south side of the island which can be plainly discerned from this city (Traverse City) on a clear day, is where the land slipped into the water. It has never grown over with bushes because it was to remain a monument to the love of Meahnonta and Wabesic.[1]

Thus was the Indian "legend," exactly as told to the readers of the *Traverse City Record-Eagle* when (the famous) Henry Ford purchased the island in 1917. Some forty-two years later newspaper editor Jay Smith admitted to the *Record-Eagle* readers that he and another inventive reporter had made the whole thing up when their editor had instructed them to fill up the front page of the newspaper with Marion Island information. A "legend" seemed to them to add interest to the island's history. Just as interesting is the fact that Smith saw his yarn repeated, as truth, several times in short histories written by others in the years to follow. In addition, a local Indian told Smith that the name assigned to the fictitious Indian princess, translated to mean *Big Skunk!*[2]

Perhaps there are even more legends or fables associated with the larger island. A scribbled account may be hidden in a mainland attic, or a faint recollection may linger in the memory of an older Native American. Legends are created, and legends are lost, like footprints along an island's shoreline.

Squaw Island — The Island of Dread — The Haunted Island

At the northeast end of the "big island" lies a high piece of ground which is occasionally separated from the main landmass by high water. In early days it was sometimes called *Squaw Island* and is the same now-and-then island which later became known as *Bassett.*

According to legend, an Indian Chief and his bride left the tiny island one day aboard their canoe. The Indian woman was never seen again, and for years the Indians who camped there left tobacco and a pipe on the ground, for her spirit when it should return to the island.[3]

Another version says that Indians held Squaw Island, "in great dread" and referred to it as *the haunted island.*[4] They never set foot on it except to place offerings to satisfy the wicked spirits who lived there. A poem by Mrs. M. E. C. Bates of Traverse City gives her version of this island of dread.[5]

I am Kabeena, a young Chippewa,
And those are our camp-fires that flicker and play
and gleam with red light athwart the black night
On the sandy shores of Grand Traverse Bay.
Here where its ruddy radiance shines
Under the shade of these dusky pines,
Sit on the sand by my side while I tell
The wonderful story of what befell
A squaw, who, a hundred years ago,
Walked where these same waves ebb and flow.

You see, up on the bay, how the Northern star
Looks down on an isle with a sandy bar
That stretches out toward the mainland shore
An arrow'd flight or a little more,
And guards its shores—a sheltering wall,
On which the white waves leap and fall.
A little isle—you can almost pace
Its whole length o'er in the moment's space
Of a whipporwill's song as he sways and swings
On a willow bough, and flirts while he sings.
There's a whispering pine with its feathery spire,
And a blasted hemlock seared by fire,
A cluster of birches white as snow
And a tangle of bushes spread below;
But never a flower in the spring is seen,
Sweet muskodeed or wintergreen,
And the wild waves wander with sob and moan
Round the little isle so sad and lone.

Well, this squaw—she was bad, yet I do not know
What she could have done that they treated her so.
But one night in the moon of the falling leaves.
When the wild wind wanders and wails and grieves
Over the hills and along the shore,

She vanished and ne'er was heard of more.
But one who watched through the misty dark
Saw the medicine men in canoes of bark,
And in their midst through the night and storm
Saw the outlines dim of a crouching form.

And then as the night passed slowly on,
In the darkest hour before the dawn,
He listened and heard from afar,
From the little isle with the sandy bar,
Like an echoing call in a weird, wild dream,
The sound of a long-drawn distant scream;
And frightened up from his weedy bed
A loon laughed loud as he swept o'er head,
A lone wolf howled on a distant hill,
a Screech owl hooted,—and all was still.
And back, ere the dark into dawn had grown,
Came the medicine men, but they came alone.

With the winter night and summer down
A hundred years have come and gone,
But the story is forgotten not
And the little isle is a gruesome spot;
For ever as comes a night of storm
There walks on its shores a fearful form,
And he who sees it is wild with dread—
Tis the wicked squaw without a head!
And over the wild waves' rush and roar
That wild death scream rings out once more.

There a white man's town at the head of the bay;
From the hillsides the forest has vanished away;
The wondering Indian starts to hear
The scream of the iron horse meet his ear;
But ever wild and lone, afar
Lies the little isle with the sandy bar.

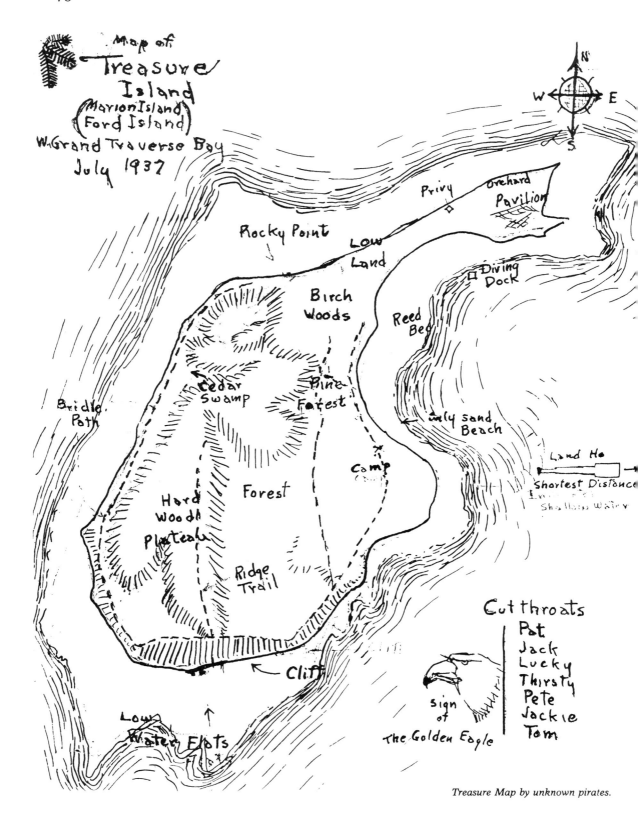

Treasure Map by unknown pirates.

Treasure Island

The haunting poem from Mrs. M. E. C. Bates' pen falls easily into the realm of intrigue so often attached to islands. Using our own imaginations, perhaps what author Bates' "bad" squaw did was to find this island's buried treasure and keep it all to herself. Where there is an island, there certainly must be a treasure. Perhaps this thought is what caused two of the employees of the former Bassett Island dance pavilion to be called "Robinson Crusoe and his man Friday." Some say a treasure was hidden on the northwest corner of the bigger island, by Mormon families who had come to the Bower's Harbor area from James J. Strang's Beaver Island community in the 1850's. If such a treasure did exist, it may still be buried beneath the ground, or hidden under a rock, or stashed in a hollow tree.

On the subject of trees, it has been said that every species of tree native to Michigan grows on the big island. Truth or fiction? Also, a key to finding the island's treasure may be in first finding three beech trees growing in a row. If the middle tree has a marlinespike* in its trunk, the treasure is hidden close by.

One fable connected to little Bassett Island tells that the island's namesake, Dick Bassett, had a unique way of keeping unwelcomed visitors away. He simply made an approaching boat sink by staring intently in its direction.

As a present-day vessel approaches this Grand Traverse Bay island gem, a welcome awaits—a time for relaxation, recreation and imagination. And, after all, isn't this invitation to fantasy part of what makes an island such a special place?

*Also called marlingspike, it is a pointed, metal spike, used for separating strands of rope while splicing.

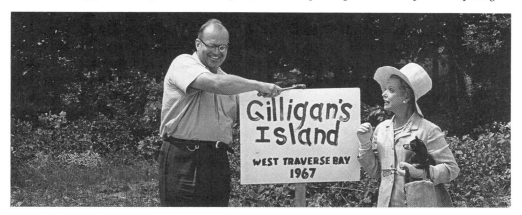

COURTESY TRAVERSE CITY RECORD-EAGLE

In 1967 a group of Traverse City "castaways" claimed the island in Grand Traverse Bay and designated it "Gilligan's Island," in honor of the popular television series. Bob Murchie represented Rennie Oil Company in temporarily renaming the island, as Natalie Schafer, an actress in the series, gave her approval.

[1]"The Legend of Marion Island," *Traverse City Record-Eagle*, 8 June, 1917, pp. 1,2.

[2]Jay Smith, "The Observer," *Traverse City Record Eagle, 29 December, 1959, p. 4.*

[3]"Our Islands," *Le Grand Traverse*, (Rouse's Book Box), p. 13.

[4]*The Traverse Region*, (Chicago: H. R. Page & Co., 1884), p. 12.

[5]Mrs. M. E. C. Bates, *The Traverse Region*, p. 12.

ENJOYING POWER ISLAND

As property of Grand Traverse County, the island beckons the mainlander to come enjoy its peaceful beauty. Such places preserved for the public offer restoration for our wilderness spirits.

Summertime on Power Island brings daytime picnics and overnight camping to those who have access by motor boats or sailboats. Hiking the shoreline or the inland trails is peaceful recreation for some, while many prefer sunbathing and swimming off the beaches of the southeastern and southern shores. Those who enjoy fishing may cast their lines for smallmouth bass in the reed grasses or for lake trout in the deep drop-offs.

A caretaker/park ranger is in residence on the island during the summer months, for the island's protection and to guide campers to the proper sites, as well as to answer visitors' questions and maintain the primitive facilities and the hiking trails. An 11:00 p.m. curfew is enforced, when everyone but the limited number of overnight campers must leave the island park. Although the total acreage of this public property is named Power Island, historic fact still clings, and the smaller land mass is sometimes called by its separate, earlier name, *Bassett Island*. On Bassett, which is a sort of overnight annex to the main island, provision has been made for camping, and it is the only spot in the whole park where this is permitted.

Some things will not be seen on Power Island. There are no buildings except for the caretaker's cabin and outbuildings and the park restrooms. There are no big marinas, only one dock for temporary moorings as supplies are unloaded.

Whitetail deer no longer live on this island, and that is probably good. Without the animals' foraging, the natural plant life on the island is making a good recovery. Although a few deer sometimes escape to the island by swimming from the mainland during the pressure of hunting season, the escapees return to their mainland habitats when the gunfire stops. A summer visitor is very unlikely to encounter a deer on Power Island. Nor will the eagle and osprey of the past be seen, since neither has yet reappeared on the island. The last, old Eagle's nest blew down from a tall tree during a 1987 summer storm.

An island visitor will not be able to buy a hot dog at the concession stand nor to visit the zoo, both having been proposed for set-up on the island park in 1976 and then quickly dismissed. Grand Traverse County Commissioner and Marion Island Advisory Board member Paul Hazelton reminded that the gift of the island to the county citizens came with restrictions on the deed "which assure it will remain a wilderness area . . ."[1]

No motor vehicles or bicycles are permitted on any of the property. Quiet walks will not be interrupted by the sights or sounds of progress, except for the hum of motor boats in the bay.

What will be found is peaceful solitude, especially away from the boat mooring and picnic areas. Without going far, a hiker can enjoy the feeling of being alone on the island.

A shoreline walk, beginning at the unloading dock on the eastern shore and first heading south, takes a visitor along several yards of sandy beach before making a quick angle and heading southwest. This sharp point, a favored picnic area, has deep water

Visitors may unload at island dock before lowering anchors nearby. PHOTO BY K. FIRESTONE

Looking toward mainland from island's east side. PHOTO BY FRED TANK

AERIAL BY PHOTAIR
View of southeastern side of Power Island on a pleasant summer day.

within fifty feet of shore. The water makes a dramatic change to very shallow and rocky as it borders the southeastern shore, and it continues to be shallow around much of the island's perimeter. Boaters should be wary. From the south beach the hiker faces Traverse City on the mainland and can wade in the city's direction for about 100 feet. Walk-

The Tank family enjoys the swimming area of the south beach.

PHOTO BY FRED TANK

South beach, looking east.

PHOTO BY K. FIRESTONE

84

ing on the sandy shore, toward the south point, the traveller looks up at a clay bluff. On this side of the diamond-shaped island, protected from the northerly winds, the tree-covered bluff has not been shaped into gentle slopes as much of the northern part of the island has. During seasons of high water, the base of the bluff erodes, causing striations of sand, gravel and clay loam to fall to the beach below. This area is very steep in places, and a few trees, also fallen from the banks, cross the visitor's shoreline walk. The smooth bark of beech trees and the white paper of the birches reflect the sun on a summer day, as they line the top of the bluff. A short distance out into the waters of the slight cove, marsh reeds invite wild ducks to swim among them. Merganzers and swans have tried nesting along this shore, but the resident raccoons and foxes quickly rob and destroy the nests.

The south point of the island is soon rounded, and the visitor no longer looks over to mainland shores of Grand Traverse County, but instead sees Leelanau County across the waters. This southern point of Power Island is a beautiful spot, with a collection of large rocks that seem to have been placed there as an explorer's resting place. The steep slope of the woodland has descended enough that hikers who wish

PHOTO BY K. FIRESTONE
Bluff along the southern shore.

PHOTO BY K. FIRESTONE
*Rocky shoreline of
the southwestern point.*

COURTESY GARY REESE
Biologist, Gary Reese, climbs access path to woodland interior.

Rocky, western shoreline, looking north.   PHOTO BY JANE NORTON

to access the inland trails may do so at this point. But the shoreland journey saves the interior of the island for later and continues its way along the beach. This natural beach is one of the good swimming locations on the island.

The northwesterly winds may ruffle the hair and cool the skin as the hiker walks this side of Power Island, some twenty miles south of where these winds have blown across Lake Michigan. The length of Grand Traverse Bay stretches to the horizon, with points along the western mainland jutting into the bay.

Further up the shoreline trail, Power Island displays large boulders, with cedar trees and pines edging the elevated, interior woodlands. A small cove, called *West Beach* on the map, leads to another inland trail, but following the cove to its north end, one finds a marshy area before reaching *North Beach.* It is on the western side of the island, about half way up the bank, that a sulphur spring has been noted in older historic accounts. A spring, perhaps the same one, has been verified by more recent explorers. The bank ascends to become the island's highest point, as it slants inland, and is scientifically referred to as *glacial drift.*

After rounding the northwestern marshy bend, the visitor will find rather mucky areas, along with a mixture of sand and small rocks and pebbles. In the spring killdeer fake their broken wings to distract the walker from their nests on the ground, and thistles, goldenrod and other flowering plants grow among the rushes and marsh grasses to bloom in late summer. The hiker is again facing Grand Traverse County and is only one-half mile from Neahtawanta Point on the mainland shore of the Old Mission Peninsula.

Marshy, northwestern shoreline, with Neahtawanta Point in background.   PHOTO BY K. FIRESTONE

GOLDENROD PHOTOS BY K. FIRESTONE

THISTLE PHOTO BY FRED TANK

Wild grapes on Bassett Island. PHOTO BY K. FIRESTONE

88

View of Bassett Island from north end of main island.   PHOTO BY K. FIRESTONE

Rounding the final bend of Power Island, its northern point, an approximately two-acre land mound comes into view. This is the high piece of ground that is usually attached by a natural causeway to the other 197 acres of Power Island. This is the ground that, in years of high water when the isthmus is covered, becomes its own separate island—the island formerly known as *Bassett Island, Squaw Island* and *The Haunted Island.* It is only haunted now by the raccoons that try to steal the contents of picnic baskets at the overnight campsites.

One historical account locates a salt spring "between the two islands, on the west side of the reef."[2] Others put the spring off the southern shore of the main island. In either place it would not be easily found, except in years of very low water. When the water is low enough to provide for the isthmus, this location acts as a "collector" of water-born seeds, where newly introduced plant species sometimes take root.[3]

The quick elevation of Bassett Island provides dry ground for five campsites, complete with picnic tables and places for staking tents. A few large trees of oak, maple, aspen and cedar, as well as their saplings, give some privacy between campsites. A short walk around the perimeter of the smaller island brings the hiker back to the connection with the bigger island.

Isthmus between the main island and Bassett Island.

1975 high water PHOTO BY
PAUL HAZELTON

1991 low water
PHOTO BY
K. FIRESTONE

A woodland trail in Power Island's interior.

PHOTO BY K. FIRESTONE

Crow's-nest look-out along northeastern shore.

PHOTO BY K. FIRESTC

At the eastern side of the pebbled isthmus, the visitor has almost completed the nearly three and one-half mile hike around Power Island. A few hundred feet of reedy, shoreline grasses make way for a small pathway. The ranger station crow's-nest lookout faces the bay and is supported some fifteen feet overhead by posts set into the sandy ground, beside the shoreline path.

This journey is over, but inland trails, through 138 acres of forest, mostly categorized as *Mesic Northern Forest,* leave many more hours of exploration and enjoyment for the serious hiker.

Not so different from the mainland, the island woodlands are mainly of maple, beech, birch, basswood, willow, oak, Norway pine and cedar. Champion trees of basswood, black willow, eastern red cedar, ironwood and rock elm have been noted on this island in Grand Traverse Bay, according to the Michigan Natural Features Inventory.[4] There are over 250 species of plants, though this is not considered to be a large number.

Dr. William Scharf, an expert on island biology, verified about 78 species of birds during his 14 explorations of Power Island, with more starlings, redstarts, ovenbirds and cardinals than are usually found on the mainland.[5] Several species of warblers are present during migration. Again, 78 is not a large number of species, but the number has increased since biologist Lee Dice made his 1923 explorations for the University of Michigan.[6] Northwestern Michigan College science instructor and island caretaker, Fred Tank, is hopeful that the American Bald Eagle will again take up residence on the island, as eagle counts are increasing in Northern Michigan and other areas.

Scharf's studies took place in 1982 and 1983, when he and area naturalist June Mason were under contract with the Nature Conservancy to construct an ecological inventory. They also found the meadow mouse, or meadow vole, which had been found on only one other Lake Michigan island, Goose Island.[7] The meadow mouse was also documented in Lee Dice's 1925 report of the observations he had made two years earlier. In order to survive, the meadow mouse needs the open fields left by logging. These open spaces on Power Island have gradually grown over through the preservation efforts of recent years. Fred Tank observed that when he began as summer caretaker of the island in 1985, "the mouse population was extremely high," but that by the summer of 1990, it had "crashed."[8] Noting these changes as normal for certain types of wildlife, Tank found this rodent population to be recovering during the summer of 1991.

Power Island has no squirrels or chipmunks, but an explorer may occasionally see a fox, ruffed grouse or muskrat. William Hurt in his *Mammals of Michigan* recorded in 1954 that the short-tailed shrew, long-tailed weasel and mink were present on the island, as well as the woodland deermouse and meadow vole, which are known to still survive there.[9] In his 1948 publication, *Island Life,* Robert Hatt stated that cottontail rabbits were present on both Marion (now Power) and South Manitou Islands.[10] Scharf found no evidence of mink or long-tailed weasel in 1982-83; and although caretaker Jack Clark spotted a cottontail on the island in 1983, none has been sighted by Fred Tank during his summers there.

Raccoons are plentiful. While entertaining the daytime visitor by eating a treat left on a picnic table, the animals can also wreak havoc by upsetting the overnight campers' supplies, robbing them of tomorrow's breakfast or other food supplies. The raccoons make their homes in the hollows of trees, safe from the human visitors.

The inland trails, some of which probably began as logging trails, and some which were cut by Ralph Matthews when he was employed as caretaker by the Rennie family during the 1960's, have been improved, maintained and added to under the direction of the island park's advisory commission, which hired Fred Tank as caretaker and guide in 1985. The wooded hiking trails measure about 15,600 feet in total length and meander up and down and across the inland terrain, as well as circling the entire island, not many yards in from the shoreline's natural paths.

PHOTO BY FRED TANK, 1991

In 1985 the Tank family began spending summers on the island, enjoying island living, as Fred Tank assumed the duties of caretaker/park ranger. L-R, back row: David, Matthew, Jason, Fred. Front row: Tina, Elizabeth, Jennifer, Alexander.

PHOTO BY FRED TANK
Alex, Jason and Elizabeth Tank and cat, Mouser, inspect a catch of rock bass.

Caretaker Fred Tank clears trails for summer visitors.   COURTESY FRED TANK

The northeastern and eastern areas of the island are lowest in elevation and contain the picnic areas and ranger's station. Eagle's Nest Lookout, named for the eagles that used to nest there, is in about the middle of the northern half of the island. At a height of about 120 feet above the shore level, the site affords nice views of the water and of the Leelanau County shoreline, to the northwest. Not far from it, the trail meanders through the marsh seeps, where cattails and other wetland plants grow. The southern path wanders atop the clay bluff and allows beautiful views of the slight cove of the south beach and of mainland Traverse City, about six miles across the water.

Eagle's Nest Lookout provides view of west arm of Grand Traverse Bay.   PHOTO BY PAUL HAZELTON

Spring mushrooms and wildflowers are a pleasing sight to the nature lover. And, on a hot summer day, the coolness of Power Island's woods brings relief when a visitor has finished the enjoyment of sandy beaches. Bright orange, red and yellow leaves and crisp autumn days brighten an opportunity to squeeze in a few more pleasant hours on the island, while the boating is still good and the sun is still high.

PHOTO BY K. FIRESTONE
Board path through marsh seeps.

PHOTO BY K. FIRESTONE
Tree hollows provide homes for the island's raccoons.

View from southern bluff trail.

Round-leaf Hepatica in April.

A time of winter stillness for Power Island.   PHOTO BY J. FIRESTONE

Perhaps the winter is the island's own time. A time for the snow to cover dormant seeds with freshness and solitude. A time of preparation for growth and renewal — renewal of this aquatic gem which invites us to return to its shores in springtime.

[1]Grand Traverse County Record of Deeds, Liber 378, p. 946.

[2]Michigan Survey Document No. 1290, Orange Risdon, 1858.

[3]June Mason, *Marion Island, Results of 1982, 1983 Plant Survey,* study commissioned by The Nature Conservancy, 1982, 1983, un-numbered first page of Summary.

[4]*Grand Traverse County Element List, Michigan Natural Features Inventory,* July, 1990.

[5]William C. Scharf, tape recorded address to Sixth Annual (combined) Meeting of the Grand Traverse Pioneer and Historical Society and the Walter Hastings Audubon Club, 17 May, 1984.

[6]*Ibid.*

[7]William H. Hurt, *The Mammals of Michigan* (Ann Arbor: The University of Michigan Press, 1954), p. 218.

[8]Fred Tank, personal interview by author, January, 1992.

[9]Hurt, pp. 103, 135, 141, 208, 218.

[10]Robert Hatt, *Island Life* (Bloomfield Hills, MI: Cranbrook Institute of Science, 1948), p. 145.

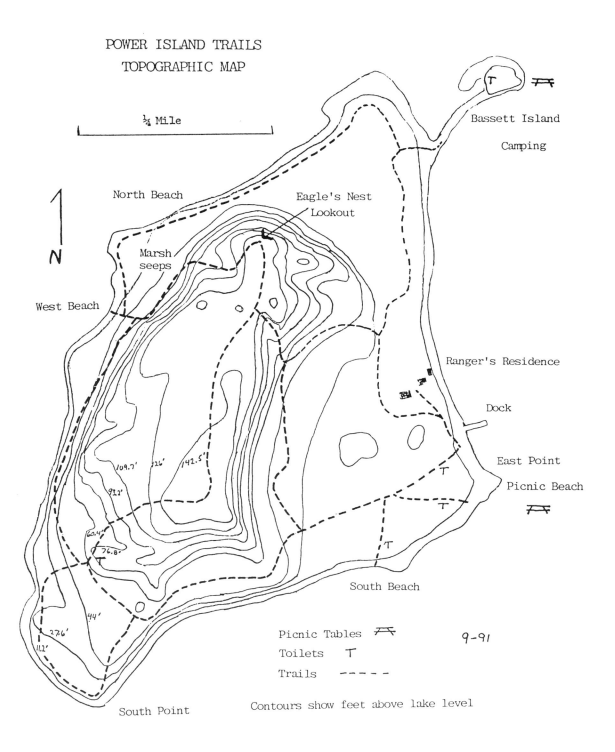

POWER ISLAND TRAILS
TOPOGRAPHIC MAP

¼ Mile

N

North Beach

West Beach

Marsh
seeps

Eagle's Nest
Lookout

Bassett Island

Camping

Ranger's Residence

Dock

East Point

Picnic Beach

109.7' *126'* *142.5'*

93.2'

60.4'

76.8'

44'

27.6'

11.2'

South Beach

South Point

Picnic Tables

Toilets   T

Trails

9-91

Contours show feet above lake level

Trail map by Fred Tank shows the many routes available to explorers.

Birds of Power Island

Compiled by Dr. William Scharf of Northwestern Michigan College
for The Nature Conservancy during 1982 and 1983

Common Loon
Great Blue Heron
Mallard
Common Merganser
Red-breasted Merganser
Killdeer
Spotted Sandpiper
Herring Gull
Ring-billed Gull
Black-billed Cuckoo
Barred Owl
Ruby-throated Hummingbird
Belted Kingfisher
Common Flicker
Yellow-bellied Sapsucker
Downy Woodpecker
Eastern Kingbird
Great Crested Flycatcher
Eastern Phoebe
Eastern Wood Pewee
Tree Swallow
Bank Swallow
Rough-winged Swallow
Barn Swallow
Blue Jay
Common Crow
Black-capped Chickadee
White-breasted Nuthatch
Red-breasted Nuthatch
Brown Creeper
House Wren
Winter Wren
Catbird
Robin
Wood Thrush

Hermit Thrush
Swainson's Thrush
Veery
Golden-crowned Kinglet
Cedar Waxwing
Starling
Red-eyed Vireo
Black-and-white Warbler
Tennessee Warbler
Nashville Warbler
Yellow Warbler
Magnolia Warbler
Black-throated Blue Warbler
Myrtle Warbler
Black-throated Green Warbler
Chestnut-sided Warbler
Bay-breasted Warbler
Blackpoll Warbler
Palm Warbler
Ovenbird
Northern Waterthrush
American Redstart
Red-winged Blackbird
Northern Oriole
Rusty Blackbird
Common Grackle
Brown-headed Cowbird
Scarlet Tanager
Cardinal
Rose-breasted Grosbeak
Indigo Bunting
American Goldfinch
White-crowned Sparrow
White-throated Sparrow
Song Sparrow

Vascular Plants of Power Island

Adapted from studies by June Mason
for the Nature Conservancy during 1982 and 1983

Horsetail Family
Field Horsetail
Thicket Horsetail

Royal Fern Family
Cut-leaved Grape Fern
Rattlesnake Fern
Cinnamon Fern
Bladder Fern
Sensitive Fern
Oak Fern
Spinulose Wood Fern
Wood Fern
Maidenhair Fair
Bracken Fern
Common Ploypod

Pondweed Family
Crisp Pondweed
Variable Pondweed
Sago Pondweed
Berchtold's Pondweed

Sedge Family
Carex plantiginea
C. Comosa
Cladium mariscoides
Scirpus atrovirens

Grass Family
Agrostis gigantia
A. Hyemalis
Elymus canadensis
Ammophilia breviligulata
Phagmites communis

Cat-tail Family
Common Cat-tail
Narrow-leaved Cat-tail

Bur-reed Family
Bur-reed

Juncaginaceae
Seaside arrow-grass

Arum Family
Jack-in-the-pulpit
Skunk-cabbage

Lily Family
Large-flowered bellwort
Wild Leek
Y. Adder's Tongue
False Solomon's Seal
Large Solomon's Seal
Starry False Solomon's Seal

Hairy Solomon's Seal
Stinking Benjamin
Large-flowered Trillium
Wild Lily-of-the-Valley

Iris Family
Blue Flag

Orchid Family
Yellow Lady's Slipper
Helleborine

Smartweed Family
Lady's Thumb
Dock-leaved Smartweed
Pale Dock
Broad-leaved Dock

Purslane Family
Spring-Beauty

Pink Family
White Campion
Rose Campion
Starry Campion
Bladder Campion
Forking Catchfly
Common Chickweed
Lesser Stitchwort

Buttercup Family
Early Meadow-rue
Common Buttercup
Wood Anemone
Canada Anemone
Goldthread
Wild Columbine
White Baneberry
Red Baneberry
Virgin's Bower

Poppy Family
Bloodroot
Dutchman's Breeches
Squirrel-corn

Mustard Family
Hoary Alyssum
Sea Rocket
Charlock
Tumble Mustard
Cut-leaved Toothwort
Lyre-leaved Rock Cress

Saxifrage Family
Foamflower
Bishops Cap
Prickly Gooseberry

Rose Family
Woodland Strawberry
Silverweed
Rough-fruited Cinquefoil
Purple Water Avens
White Avens
Agrimony
Smooth Rose
Rugosa Rose
Pin Cherry
Black Cherry
Chokeberry
High-Bush Blackberry
Wild Red-Raspberry
Black Raspberry
Juneberry

Bean Family
White Sweet Clover
Yellow Sweet Clover
Least Hop Clover
Beach Pea
Marsh Pea

Geranium Family
Herb-Robert

Spurge Family
White Spurge

Touch-me-not Family
Spotted Touch-me-not

St. John's Wort Family
St. John's Wort

Violet Family
Canadian White Violet
Small White Violet
Downy Yellow Violet
Common Blue Violet
Long-Spurred Violet
Sweet White Violet

Evening Primrose Family
Fireweed
Evening-primrose
Enchanter's nightshade

Ginseng Family
Wild Sarsaparilla

Parsley Family
Sweet Cicely
Queen Anne's Lace

(continued)

Heath Family
Indian Pipe
Creeping Snowberry
Bearberry
Blueberry

Primrose Family
Star-flower

Dogbane Family
Spreading Dogbane

Milkweed Family
Common Milkweed
Swamp Milkweed

Borage Family
Common Hound's Tongue
Small Forget-me-not

Vervane Family
Blue Vervain

Mint Family
Wild Mint
Peppermint
Water Horehound
Motherwort
Heal-all
Ground-ivy
Catnip
Common Skullcap
Mad-dog Skullcap
Wild Basil
Dotted Monarda
Big Blue Hyssop

Nightshade Family
Climbing Nightshade

Figwort Family
Common Mullein
P. Gerardia
Cow-wheat
Wood-betony

Broomrape Family
Neech-drops

Madder Family
Sweet-scented Bedstraw
Sticky Bedstraw
Northern Bedstraw
Partridge Berry

Honeysuckle Family
Twinflower
Common Elderberry
Red-Berried Elderberry
Bush Honeysuckle
Tartarian Honeysuckle

Blue Bell Family
Brook Lobelia

Phytolaccaceae
Pokeweed

Stonecrop Family
Sedum

Urticaceae
Stinging Nettle
Slender Nettle

Composite Family
Joe-pye Weed
Boneset
White Snakeroot
Slender Fragrant Goldenrod
Grass-leaved Goldenrod
Early Goldenrod
Gray Goldenrod
Showy Goldenrod
Rough-stemmed Goldenrod
Canadian Goldenrod
White Aster
Large-leaved Aster
Small White Aster
Daisy Fleabane
Pussy's Toes
Clammy Everlasting
Pearly Everlasting
Stick-tight
Yarrow
Wormwood
Common Burdock
Bull Thistle
Canada Thistle
Spotted Knapweed
Yellow Goat's-beard
Purple Salsify
Dandelion
Red-Seeded Dandelion
Wild Lettuce
Tall Rattlesnake Weed
Orange Hawkweed
Hairy Hawkweed
King Devil
Burdock
Prickly Lettuce
Hairy Lettuce
Smooth Hawk's Beard
Sow Thistle

Pine Family
Balsam Fir
White Spruce
Eastern Hemlock

Yew Family
Yew

Cypress Family
Prostrate Juniper
Northern White Cedar

Maple Family
Boxelder
Moose Maple
Red Maple
Sugar Maple

Alder Family
Speckled Alder

Birch Family
Yellow Birch
Paper Birch
Ironwood

Honeysuckle Family
Bush Honeysuckle
Tartarian Honeysuckle

Staff-Tree Family
Bittersweet

Dogwood Family
Alternate-leaved Dogwood
Round-leaved Dogwood
Red-osier Dogwood

Beech Family
American Beech
Red Oak

Ash Family
White Ash
Green Ash

Witch-hazel Family
Witch-hazel

Mulberry Family
White Mulberry

Buckthorn Family
Common Buckthorn

Cashew Family
Poison Ivy
Staghorn Sumac

Legume Family
Black Locust

Willow Family
Beaked Willow
Sandbar Willow
Silky Willow
Bigtooth Aspen
Quaking Aspen
Balsam Poplar

Oleaster Family
Buffalo-berry

Linden Family
American Basswood

Elm Family
American Elm
Rock Elm

Grape Family
Summer Grape
Riverbank Grape

BIBLIOGRAPHY

BOOKS

Bates, M. E.C. and Buck, M. K. *Along Traverse Shores.* Traverse City, MI: 1891.

Blackbird, Andrew. *History of the Ottawa and Chippewa Indians of Michigan.* Ypsilanti: Ypsilanti Job Printing House, 1887.

Craker, Ruth. *First Protestant Mission in the Grand Traverse Region.* 1935; reprint. Mount Pleasant: Rivercrest House, 1979.

Davis, Marion M. *Island Stories.* ed. George N. Fuller. Lansing: State Printers, 1947.

Fuller, George N. ed. *Historic Michigan. Vol. 3, National Historical Association, Inc.*

Fuller, S. M., *Summer On The Lakes.* Boston: Charles C. Little and James Brown, 1844.

Hatt, Robert T. *Island Life.* Bloomfield Hills, Mich.: Cranbrook Institute of Science, 1948.

Hurt, William H. *The Mammals of Michigan.* Ann Arbor: The University of Michigan Press, 1954.

La Grand Traverse, Traverse City Public Schools, student project, 1947.

Leach, M. L. *A History: Grand Traverse Region.* Traverse City, Mich., 1883. Reprints from The Grand Traverse Herald.

Noble, Percy. *Noble Memories.* Traverse City, Mich.: The Pioneer Study Center, 1981.

Page, H. R. *The Traverse Region.* 1884; reprint. The Grand Traverse Pioneer and Historical Society, 1991.

Polk's Traverse City and Grand Traverse County Directory, 1921-22. Detroit: R. L. Polk & Company, 1921.

Schoolcraft, Henry J. *Narrative Journal of Travels — during 1820.* Mentor L. Williams, ed. East Lansing: Michigan State College Press, 1953.

Sprague, Elvin L. *Sprague's History of Grand Traverse and Leelanaw Counties,* Michigan. B. F. Bowen, 1903.

Standard Atlas of Grand Traverse County, Michigan. Chicago: Geo. A. Ogle & Co., 1908.

Strang, James J. *Ancient and Modern Michilimackinac.* Beaver Island, 1854; reprint, Mackinac Island, Mich.: W. Stewart Woodfill, 1959.

Wakefield, Lawrence and Lucille. *Sail & Rail.* Traverse City: Village Press, 1980.

Williams, A. V. ed. *Currents Of The Boardman,* Grand Traverse Historical Society, 1982.

NEWSPAPERS

The Grand Traverse Herald 2/24/1881
                  10/19/1889

The Traverse Bay Eagle 12/9/1898

The Traverse City Evening Record 5/4, 5/14 & 6/29/1906,
                             3/27, 6/17, 7/10, 8/2 & 8/5, 1907

The Traverse City Record Eagle

8/15/1914	2/11, 8/13/1970
6/ 8/1917	7/12/1972
8/11/1921	10/15, 11/15 & 12/26/1974
8/17/1923	5/2, 5/7, 5/14, 7/22, 7/29, 7/30,
7/17, 7/18, 7/19 & 7/21/1924	8/1, 8/6, 8/7, 8/20, 9/24, 9/25,
2/19/1931	10/15 & 7/23/1975
12/12/1934	1/24, 1/29, 1/30, 5/22, 5/27
4/14/1941	& 9/20/1976
10/11/1944	3/26, 4/13, 9/10 & 9/20/1977
10/28/1953	6/14/1979
10/28, 11/7/1959	5/27/1983
2/26/1966	
4/22, 8/19/67	

PUBLIC RECORDS

Grand Traverse County — Record of Deeds, several
                        Book of Miscellaneous Records, No. 3
                        Board of Commissioners Resolutions
                        No. 48-75 and No. 138-86

Michigan Survey Document No. 1290

OTHER

Colton, J. H. *Colton's Tourist Map of the Great Lakes,* New York, 1862, at Clarke Historical Library, Central Michigan University, Mount Pleasant, Michigan.

Grand Traverse Pioneer and Historical Society, tape recording of Sixth Annual (combined) Meeting with the Walter Hastings Audubon Club, May, 1984.

Hazelton, Paul, *Queen Mary Ship's Log,* 1978.

Kroupa, Nynetta. *Marion Island,* TS., 1928, in the Grand Traverse Pioneer and Historical Society Archives.

Mason, June. *Marion Island, Results of 1982, 1983 Plant Survey,* study commissioned by The Nature Conservancy, 1982, 1983.

Michigan Natural Features Inventory, *Grand Traverse County Element List,* July, 1990.

Reese, Gary, et al. *A Natural Areas Inventory of Grand Traverse County, Michigan,* Lansing: Michigan Department of Natural Resources, April, 1990.

Rennie, Ferris J. *Wren's Nest Ship's Log,* 1961. (Vessel spelling was Ren's Nest.)

Whipp, Donald V., Jr. *Marion Island, West Arm of Grand Traverse Bay,* property appraisal, 1968.

INDEX